M000044158

When She Stopped Asking Why….

A Mother's Journey Through Teen Substance Abuse and the Loving Path to Finding her Clarity, Courage and Purpose

When She Stopped Asking Why: A Mother's Journey Through Teen Substance Abuse and the Loving Path to Finding her Clarity, Courage and Purpose Copyright © 2017 by Marsha Vanwynsberghe

All rights reserved. No part of this book may be used or reproduced in any manner whatsoever without written permission except in the case of brief quotations in critical articles or reviews.

Disclaimer: The information in this book is for educational purposes only and does not constitute legal or any other advice in any way. Readers should consult with their own trusted advisors before embarking on any life changing endeavours.

Published by Prominence Publishing.
www.prominencepublishing.com

Marsha Vanwynsberghe can be reached as follows:
www.marshavanw.com

ISBN: 978-1-988925-05-9

First Edition: October 2017

Cover Photography and Author Photo by Hilary Gauld-Camilleri.
http://hilarygauld.com

Final image in this book is courtesy of Cheryl Carter, photographed by Linda Thomson

This book is dedicated to my boys, my greatest teachers, to my husband who gives me space to be me, to my tribe of amazing warrior women and to my faith that it is possible to get to the other side of tragedy.

Foreword

This book has been in the making for a number of years. It took time for me to heal, to shift, to grow and to build the confidence to be able to share my story. It took even longer for me to understand the importance of sharing my story with the rest of the world.

I spent years stuck in a simple question... "Why me, why them, and why us?" The word WHY defined my entire life for many years. I couldn't stop focusing on the word WHY. Then it hit me. There was no answer that would give me any degree of satisfaction. It was a redundant question that kept me stuck as a victim, and I was done living as a victim. In fact, I was exhausted and desperately searching for change, for space and freedom from the pressure of hiding my story in my everyday life. I had no idea that changing my questions would ultimately change my life.

The years spent crawling through quicksand, climbing hills and mountains and trying to hide from the world was exhausting. I know that I was never really hiding. Everyone knew what was going on in our family. It hadn't been a secret for many years. I had to grow as a person first to be able to handle and hold the magnitude of this problem. I took years to decide to let go of that weight and then allow myself to be transparent and authentic with the world. From the outside, it may have looked easy and fast; trust me, I was moving at a snail's pace doing the cha-cha in my life.

Through this process, I learned how to heal, to grow, to shift my mindset, to make sense out of the chaos, to forgive others and myself, and most importantly to accept that the only thing I could control in this crazy world was myself. My thoughts, my actions, my reactions and ultimately what I decided to do with my life. were all mine to own. The WHAT became far more important than the WHY.

I dedicate this process to my wonderful husband Brad, and to all of the amazing girlfriends and family members who have stayed by my side during an incredibly painful growth process. I am grateful for the friends who stayed, the ones who were there when I didn't ask for help, the ones who completely walked away and the new ones who entered my life. I honour every single one of you, because you have played a massive role in who I am today.

My story is for all the Moms who lost themselves while raising their kids, to all the parents who've struggled with their children and with themselves and to anyone else who is hiding from the world because their shame is driving the wheel. No matter what pile of crap you are fighting your way through, no matter what you are resisting, no matter how much pain you have experienced, I acknowledge you, I honour you and I promise that you are not alone in your suffering. No matter what your story, you aren't now and you never have been. I am in your corner, I am your voice and I will help you to find your voice. I am here to believe in you because you don't believe in yourself…. YET.

My wish is that my story will spark something in you. A spark of hope, a light, a glimmer of belief, or a complete shift in your mindset. You are capable of more than you realize. You are here for a reason, you have a voice, you have unique gifts, you have a purpose and I am very grateful for you.

Thank you for reading and sharing in my story. It's not my story. It is our story.

Table of Contents

Introduction

<u>"My Story, Not Theirs"</u>

Parenting is the craziest, scariest roller coaster ride I have ever been on. It's been a crash course with no manual and no idea of what to do half of the time. It's ok, because I had it all planned out. I was going to have healthy, happy kids, and a life full of opportunities, love, memories and possibilities.

Life had a very different plan for me. A plan I didn't ask for, didn't want, but it was what I was given. I pray that you never have to walk in my shoes. If you do, please remember you are not alone.

After spending many years hiding, angry at the world, and resenting our circumstances, in fact resenting our life, I knew something had to change. I knew the anger and emotions were truly only hurting me and my family. It was not changing anything in my world or in theirs. It was as though our family was in a rowboat, with each of us rowing in different directions, stuck, going in circles, and I was holding onto the anchor. I was drowning, trying to save everyone, and spending all my energy controlling something that I had zero control over. I had to let go, to trust and to surrender. It was truly the only way. Surrendering was the only option I had left. I had tried everything else that I could think of. Everything except taking care of me. I simply decided to change.

Through the process of growth and change, I found my voice and my purpose. I found it when I wasn't looking for it. I decided to share my story. This is my story, not theirs. The heartbreaking story of a parent dealing with teen substance abuse at a level far past "normal" experimentation. Now I am most passionate about helping parents find their clarity, confidence and courage in order to find their strength and peace in their crazy life. I am driven to help women find their voice, take back their power in their life, to do what lights them up, to own what they can control and have the freedom to explore a new relationship with their partner/spouse.

The story was chaotic and the primary lesson was simple. As parents, caregivers and friends, we are not here to fix or change others. We are here to lead ourselves. To be the best version of us that we can be. Not the version everyone thinks we should be. Not the version that matches the expectations of others. The version that we are designed to be. The one that is full of our unique gifts, talents and skills. The person who is here to impact and influence change in this world. That version must come out of hiding. It is a waste of God given resources to leave it untapped.

I am driven to assist others in finding the gifts in their adversities...the hidden gifts that are tightly wrapped up in their challenges. Unveiling those gifts becomes the first step in finding our way through the adversity. Staring at the problem, trying to make it easier, or avoiding it, never changes the issue. It is possible to get to the other side. When you are ready. When you decide that you no longer choose to be in the same place for one minute longer. Not one minute, one hour, one day, one week or month. When you make that decision, you will find the doors of opportunity. They've been there all along.

We spend most of our lives in this long hallway full of closed doors. The doors represent different moments and opportunities in our lives. We spend so long looking at the doors, trying to decide which door is the best for us, which door is perfect, which one has the least amount of pain, which one will bring us the most ease, that we rarely open any of the doors. We just sit there in fear hoping the answer will come to us. It doesn't.

Answers never come when we are standing still. The answers come when we are in action. When we open a door. There will be heartache, pain and frustration behind every single door. There will also be beauty, growth and happiness behind every door. And each door will bring another door. There is no perfect door. The doors represent our choices and our choices create how our life unfolds. Life will happen no matter what, and time will pass by regardless whether we stand still and watch it or if we actively participate in our life. We always get to choose. Once I owned the power of the word 'choice,' I could see that I had a choice all along. We all do.

I am openly sharing my story and hoping it helps you with yours. Your story is just that...a story. A story that you have identified with and subscribed to for far too long. I pray that my story will remind you that you always have a choice in your life. You have had it all along, you simply forgot to exercise your right to own your choice.

Through my workshops, speaking engagements, events, and books, I am here to gently remind you that you do have control over your own life. No matter what your starting point is, you are always one decision away from creating change in your life. One decision, one action, and one step at a time.

Chapter One

<u>Owning it ALL</u>

"Owning our story can be hard, but not nearly as difficult as spending our lives running from it"

Brene Brown

For many years all I could see was darkness. My days were full of few smiles, little happiness and dread for what the next moment would bring. I was stuck in a vicious cycle of replaying past events, trying to change them, and living in utter fear for what the future would bring for our family. The thought of living in the present was nauseating because it was a harsh reality to what we were facing. There was nowhere for my brain to go; hence, there was nowhere for my thoughts to go either. Just a roller coaster/hamster wheel ride that seemed impossible to change. I was strapped in, fighting for my life and I couldn't figure out how to stop the ride.

I have always been a very realistic and positive person. I would give you a straight up answer for anything. I had no problem saying it like it is. The problem was it was now my life that was spinning out of control and I couldn't figure out the "right" advice to save my life.

I hated where my mindset was and in fact I hated where my life was in general. For a period of time I hated God for giving me this life, which led me to hate myself for such terrible thoughts. I knew something had to change. I started listening to guided meditations, You-Tube videos, podcasts, anything motivational to shift my mindset. I then came across Brene Brown's Ted Talk on Vulnerability. Her message hit me as though she was speaking directly to me. I started to come to grips with owning my own story. It was real. There was no hiding from it any longer. In fact, the longer I hid from it, the more it controlled me, the more power it had over me. I didn't realize I was the one that was giving it so much power. My story was dictating every single aspect of my life. I was intrigued with the concept of owning my own story and what that meant.

My interpretation of owning my own story means coming to a place where I can understand what my role is in the situation and what someone else's role is in the situation. In other words, learning how to own everything that is mine to own. That includes: my behaviour, my reaction, my attitude, my mindset in how I handle and react to everything that occurs around me. In owning my own story I clearly understood what part was my story and what wasn't mine to own.

This was a critical first step. I believe it's important to own my own story, no matter what the story, because it means taking responsibility for my own life and taking ownership for how I choose to live it and what I do with it. I believe that it is allowing me to be in a place of not blaming somebody else for where my life is at and ultimately taking responsibility for what I can control.

I started to understand the importance of owning my story, but I couldn't figure out how I could possibly share it with others. What would they think? What would they say? Everyone would obviously blame us for the problems in our family, because subconsciously I couldn't help but still blame myself. A mom is supposed to keep her kids safe, protect them from harm, and guide them into adulthood with a life full of potential opportunities. I felt like such a failure as a mom, a wife and a human being.

Drugs entered our household when our kids were only 12 and 13 years old. I was very sick at this time with a blood staph infection after years of repeated surgeries. This is when we found marijuana for the first time. It likely isn't the first time it was used, just the first time it was found. I have no doubt that we made many mistakes along the way, but I can say that I was always clear that it was not ok for them to use drugs and definitely not to be found in our house. My message never swayed, no matter how many times we found it.

This "problem" never went away. No matter what we did. We grounded, we took away privileges, removing sporting privileges and eventually living arrangements. It still never went away.

This was something I did not see coming because before the drugs surfaced we were what I would consider a very happy family, the four of us. We were a very active family; the boys were both active in different sports. We spent a lot of time with extended family and had a tremendous number of friends. We're very social people and we had a lot of fun together. There wasn't anything that critically went wrong in order for this to start to happen in our life. It was a big shock when it first started. People who knew what was going on would pass along their advice and judgment... "It's just a phase, be more strict, why don't you do something, just tell them no." There was no shortage of advice from others.

My first reaction was anger and confusion because I couldn't understand it. I was exposed to alcohol as a young child, and I saw drugs many times as a teen. It was just something I never even experimented with and never wanted anything to do with so I had a hard time accepting it being in my home and part of my kid's lives. That was my first reaction. I was desperately trying to fix the problem, trying to stop it all while trying to hide our story from the world. The more I tried to stop it, the worse it got. It never slowed down or stopped showing up in our home.

During these early years, I felt like I was living a double life because we didn't share what was going on with our friends or family until almost two years later. It was out of pure shame that we hid – we were ashamed because we were upset about the frequent drug use, and embarrassed at our inability as parents to stop it. That is just where my mind was at during this point in my life. As a society, we equate kids' behaviour to how well a parent does their job. It's a universal "unspoken" law. When you see a child throw a temper tantrum, the first thing you do is look at the parents. Or when a child is well behaved because they sit still, we think the parents did a great job of raising their kids. There comes a point in time when we must acknowledge that our kids have their own brain and they will make their own decisions and every single decision has its own consequence.

I wanted to hide our story, thinking the "phase" would eventually pass. I am not proud of my thought patterns and how I did or didn't handle it. I think I reacted the way that I did because shame and embarrassment were controlling my life. I was far more obsessed with the judgment of others then I ever thought I would be. I also recognize that these concerns did nothing to fix our situation. It was a massive waste of energy.

Not that I would go back and change how I did react because from the very beginning I made it clear that drugs were not allowed in our house. I did not want it as part of our life and I was persistent that they could do more in their life and become more than drugs would allow. I was consumed with what other people would think and I was afraid of how it would make me look as a parent in the eyes of others. I was so scared for their future too. The path that they were on, the frequency of their use and how it was changing them as people. All of it had me so scared for their future and if they would even have one.

The other critical piece is that I have dedicated my entire life and career working as a health and fitness expert. I spent my life – 25 years working with people to help them make physical, emotional and transformational changes in their life. How could I possibly do that and have such a mess in my own personal life? I felt like such a hypocrite. It took every ounce of energy I had to "fake" my happiness in my life while I was with my clients. They didn't come to see me to hear complaining and drama. My emotions were out of control by this point and when I spoke of our story, I would break down in tears. I wasn't ready yet, not even close. At this point in my life I was owning everyone else's actions, and tearing myself apart for not having the answers to fix it. It was a vicious circle that I couldn't break.

It didn't take long to realize that we had a real problem on our hands. Life started becoming very unpredictable, or extremely predictable depending which way you looked at it. There were signs of drugs everywhere and constantly. Drugs became the number one source of our fights and arguments in our house.

We never knew what the weekend would bring. Saturdays, Sundays, holidays, summer break, March break, any days that were considered a "break" by the rest of society, were a nightmare for us. We lost all aspect of our lives. We were completely under the control of what chaos drugs would bring to our home on any given day. It interfered with everything and it consumed our life. It started to affect them in their personality, their progress in school and they were slowly becoming someone else. We were losing them. It was like watching a horrible movie that we couldn't turn off or stop watching. It was no movie. It was our everyday life.

At one point, approximately 12-18 months into their experimentation, they stopped going to school, they stopped functioning in any normal part of society. So many times they would say, "well so and so is doing it too," and our answer was always the fact that it didn't matter to us. I didn't care what the "other kids" were doing. My boys needed to function in society and they weren't. It crossed a line at one point where they weren't functioning in any part of what I would call normal.

At this time, I started searching for answers, solutions and help for our family. There was no doubt that this was quickly becoming a massive problem for our boys and our family.

It started with marijuana, their gateway drug, and it eventually progressed to other drugs such as meth, ecstasy and many other things that we never knew about. This correlated to the time period when school attendance drastically dropped, and eventually they stopped going completely.

One of our biggest issues is that they became each other's enabler and they could hide it from us and blame it on each other. It became even more difficult because both boys were involved at the same time.

Around the second year into it, I really started to reach out to counselling – I didn't know where to go. We tried a few different counsellors and I finally found some that worked for me and could help me to understand our situation. I found a parent support group for my husband and I to attend. This was a critical step for us because it really helped us to understand that we didn't create this, we didn't start it and we could only choose how we handled it. That became the first step of owning my own story because in doing so I realized what was and wasn't mine to own. We had tried so many things to stop this cycle and instead it just grew and grew.

Drugs tore our family unit apart completely. It took away years of happiness that we will never get back. I feel like it stole our boys' youth and it stole their unique potential and capabilities. At the time, it turned them into different people. It affected their brains, it affected their learning capacity, and it

affected their personalities. I watched my very loving boys become aggressive and very scary at times
when they were either high or we had found drugs.
I didn't know who they were becoming anymore. It
literally tore us all apart.

At this time, approximately 2.5 years into our story,
we decided it was time to share it with extended family members. We couldn't hide it or come up with any
more excuses as to why the boys weren't around or
why they were missing holidays. Major issues were
starting to arise, such as legal issues with the police.
It was a painful time because we were 2.5 years into
this experience and our family was 2.5 years behind
us. Their reactions were things we went through in
the beginning but they had just learned of the information. They were processing and not blaming but
trying to find reasons why this happened. There were
no reasons, no logical reasons for this mess in our
lives.

Honestly, it was impossible to hide any longer. Looking
back, I wish we had reached out sooner. That is one
of my regrets. Living the way that we did only contrib-
uted to our feelings of being alone in our pain.

I felt relieved when I shared the story. To be honest, the
more we started to share it the more I wanted to share
it. I started to feel better because I felt like the ton of
bricks that I had been carrying, that was weighing me
down, was finally being released, one at a time. They

weren't mine to hold and carry because they weren't my choices. Sharing it with other family members was a start, a first step and then we started to share with some close friends. In all honesty, a lot of people suspected what was happening.

Through the sharing process, I finally understood the phrase, "Owning your own story." To me, this phrase means that I own my part; I own my life, I own my choices, what I choose to do with my life and how I react to it. The reason why I think it's so important is because it sets an example that my boys are going to have to own their own story in order to change it and to do something different. I can't own that and take that away from them, it's theirs to own. That's one of the biggest reasons why I feel so confident and sure that this is how I have to proceed moving forward to live, is because it's what everyone will have to do as well.

I didn't happen overnight. It was and is a work in progress that got a little bit easier every single time I shared. I spent a lot of time writing, reading, trying to find positive information, and trying to find ways to let go of my anger. I was very angry for a long time. I carried that weight for many years. I was weighed down with anger and resentment. In the process of writing, counselling, reading, and meditating, it became a collection of exercises that really helped me to recognize that I had truly done everything possible. I was at the end of my rope. The only thing left to do was to let go of the rope, to truly surrender the "control" that I didn't have in the first place.

This level of acceptance, the point of surrendering was a point that I resisted. I believed that surrendering was the same as quitting and I was not a quitter. I am a fighter. I have been a fighter all of my life. I never backed down from a challenge or from anyone for that matter. The problem was that being a fighter wasn't working and there were no winners in this situation. I couldn't figure out what to do to fix it, to change our story. Everything I tried backfired and did the exact opposite. I kept replaying the events over and over in my head. I kept thinking if I did this differently or that differently that we would have different results. In hindsight, I could look back and realize that there wasn't anything more that I could do; we were reaching the fork in the road. Something had to change, none of us we were going to survive on this path.

"On every journey you take, you face choices.
At every fork in the road, you make a choice.
And it is those decisions that shape our lives."

Mike DeWine

There were a number of turning points, which I referred to as a fork in the road. There were a few specific points in time where I finally embraced that this problem with drugs was no longer a "small issue." In 2013, I found out that my older son was running drugs for his friends, which I didn't even know what that was at the time. I was so naïve. The police caught him red-handed in our house and instead of chastising him, they laughed it off and said, "We know we'll be back here again."This was a turning point because I felt that we were fighting this battle alone, and it became clear that we were the only ones who had issues with the drug use. The police didn't seem to care and neither did the schools. All we were told was that "everyone's hands were tied because they were minors." No one had any solutions or suggestions and no one had any control over them. The only advice we were given was "pray that we make it until they're 18 years old and adults." That was stellar advice for a mom trying to save her kids. Our boys were truly untouchable and they knew it. It was impossible to convince kids to try and change something when there's no repercussions, consequences or reasons to change.

Later that year became another turning point in my life. One morning I came home early from work and I found yet another baggie of marijuana in the house. I tried to flush it down the toilet. I ended up in a very scary situation on my own with the boys. I was really afraid they would hurt me, and for one of the first times I felt scared for my safety. That became an eye opener that I really had to do something differently and this was a much bigger problem. I was scared to be in my home by myself.

I am a very feisty, independent, strong willed and stubborn person and most people who know me would attest to that. Finding myself in that moment was as unbearable because I could never figure out in what universe would I ever agree to allow myself to be in that situation!

This is painful to share because at this point in my story, I don't believe that my boys were there anymore. When I looked at them I didn't see them anymore. I saw who they were becoming: complete strangers to me. Drugs were calling all the shots. All of them. I was fighting an entity that had a life of its own and it was slowly dividing and controlling all of us.

I felt the pull to share it publicly for a number of reasons. Seeing so many people struggling in private, so many families feeling broken, people living in shame, guilt and blame for choices that weren't their own, I felt called to be a voice. It's hard to explain, I knew with certainty that this was part of my story. Being a voice for families who were affected by teen substance abuse became my purpose. As I started to work through my own process, I continually came across other people and families who were in very similar circumstances. Actually, I found myself connected to Facebook groups, people from long distances and families in my own city. Literally thousands of people who were struggling with the same issues in their homes, and virtually all in private. For the first time, I realized that I wasn't alone, not even close.

The one consistent message I heard was that everyone was too scared to talk. They were afraid of what everyone else was going to think of them, how they would be judged by others. They simply wanted to bury it, suffer in silence and make it go away. Except it doesn't go away. I felt called to be a voice for others. I knew that I wanted to go first and share my story as a parent dealing with substance abuse at this level with their teens in their home. I decided to share to help other parents learn to surrender, let go of their anger, to own their part of the story and let go of everything else.

Their story didn't have to define them any longer. They did not fail as a parent. Even though to this day I still struggle with this statement. I repeatedly asked myself, "Did I fail as a parent?"

Then I would repeat the mantra I wrote for myself:

> **"I never bought it for them, I never gave it to them, and I tried everything humanly possible to stop it."**

The more I tried to own their choices in life, the less likely they would own their own choices. We couldn't both own them at the same time. Honestly, we are all responsible for owning our own choices in life. That is the first step we must take in order to create change in any area of our lives. That's what helps me to own my own story and to move forward in my life.

The more people I find along the way that need help, the more I feel the need to keep going and it fuels me. It actually fuels and supports me. I believe it's also helping me to grow and heal myself in more ways than I imagined it was possible. It was time to take back control of my own life. I was ready to write a brand new ending to my story.

> *"When we deny the story, it defines us. When we own the story, we can write a brand new ending."*
>
> **Brene Brown**

Chapter Two

<u>My Values Create My Boundaries</u>

"Daring to set boundaries is about having the courage to love ourselves even when we risk disappointing others."

Brene Brown

Everyone had advice for us – family, friends, support groups and counsellors. The most consistent advice we kept hearing was to "set boundaries and follow through." We had created so many sheets of rules to follow, and put so many guidelines in place that eventually it became a joke. No matter what we set, they wouldn't follow through or we struggled to follow through with the consequences. It was hard, harder than I can put into words. At this point our boys were between 15 and 16 years old and we were running out of options as parents while the issues surrounding drugs kept escalating.

I had to find a way to create a change. My personal safety was becoming a real issue. I was suffocating. My anxiety was out of control, and all I wanted to do was hide from the world. Yet I had nowhere to go, because my home was no longer my salvation. I no longer wanted to be in my home. It wasn't feeling safe for me to be there without my husband because it became inevitable that I would be finding and dealing with drugs in our home.

Creating space was a huge learning experience that I had to go through because I didn't have any space. If I was not home, I was putting on a fake smile, trying to say I'm happy, and everything was normal. My job required me to work with clients one-on-one. It was getting harder to pretend that things were going well. I had no space at work and I had no space at home. No space to breathe, space for peace, or space to find an ounce of happiness.

I felt very alone at this point in my life. My husband and I were drowning. There was little peace or joy anywhere. Life was full of dread and fear. Fear of the weekend, fear of the next phone call, fear of what would go wrong and fear of even coming home.

I was struggling to reach out to anyone, afraid of the judgment of others. I was still in the mindset that felt I had to fix this problem because I was their mother and I took this role as it was mine to fix.

I worked close to home and initially my husband commuted long distances, so he was away for most of the day. That was his first job when this chaos started, and he eventually lost that job which only compounded all of the stress in our home. His second job during this time period also involved long distance commuting, so I felt like this weighed on me, because he had to stay at work. We couldn't risk him being distracted and affecting his job. That meant that I would be in the thick of it all day long. I was truly suffocating. There was very little space for me and I felt very much alone, lost and afraid. I had no life anymore, nothing that was my own that didn't revolve around my boys. Honestly, I felt like they had high-jacked my entire life. Something had to change because I was honestly hating every aspect of my life, and I equally hated feeling this way. I was normally a very positive, driven and loving person and I hated who I was becoming.

I started to do some reading on personal boundaries. The definition of the word "boundary" hit home with me.

> *"A boundary is a definite place where your responsibility ends and another person's begins. It stops you from doing things for others that they should be doing for themselves. A boundary also prevents you from rescuing someone from the consequences of their destructive behaviour that they need to experience in order to grow."*
>
> *Melody Beattie*

This definition literally stopped me in my tracks. I had zero boundaries! I was owning and taking full responsibility for the choices of my kids, even though it was 100% outside of my control. That was ridiculous! This definition became a game changer in my life.

I started to be conscious about the environment I was living in. Was I around positive people? Before our life took this turn, I really prided myself on spending time with positive, optimistic people with great energy. I didn't just spend time with people of that mindset, I surrounded myself with these people. That described my boundaries in the outside world. My inside world was drastically different. At home I had no boundaries whatsoever because my kids were still minors and I had very little I could do to protect those boundaries.

My boundaries started to become about my safety. That's when things really started to shift for me. We had rules in our house. I thought rules and boundaries were the same thing for a long time. Rules were general rules of the home, such as curfew, school, and chores.

Boundaries were very different from rules. Boundaries became the line that would dictate my actions. For example, if I felt threatened, unsafe, or disrespected, that became my cue to immediately do something differently. I would leave home, phone the police or call for help. My personal boundaries became part of my values and they dictated my actions.

Creating personal boundaries was one of the first steps to finding clarity. I started to learn some simple things that I had to do to protect my boundaries. The police explained how I had to carry my phone fully charged in my coat. I carried my car keys with me so that I could get out of the house quickly. I carried my purse around my body. Honestly, it's mind blowing, but that was my life at that time in our lives. I needed to be able to quickly and safely get out of the house if necessary.

I felt like a victim in my own home and I had allowed myself to become one. The more clear I became on what those boundaries were, the easier it became to handle the unpredictable situations. A few examples of boundaries in our home included:

- No drugs or paraphernalia in our home
- No damaging property
- No personal threats and
- No lack of respect

The boundaries were written and signed in order to live in our house. That's the level we were at in that moment of time in our house.

There were times that the police were there every day for a week. Sometimes twice a day. The police and the counsellors told us to keep calling the police for support, even though nothing would happen. It seemed ridiculous but there were no options left. Many times I wondered what was the point of calling the police repeatedly because nothing was happening and nothing was changing. I would simply remind myself that it was not a safe environment and that dictated my actions.

I hit so many barriers. It was nonstop. The main barrier I faced was the fact that they were minors and according to the law, a minor under 16 cannot be asked to leave your home. Between the ages of 13-16, legally, very little happens to minors. There are years where you have no recourse and no rights as a parent whatsoever. As a parent, you bear all the responsibilities if they are in trouble or if they cause trouble. I couldn't believe the constant spiral. I felt like I was fighting the rules of society, the police, the laws and still trying to fix what was happening with our boys. I felt more than lost, I felt stranded in my own life.

During this time, I asked for tremendous support. I would phone Crime Stoppers and the police on a regular basis. I finally made my way up to the chief of police and to the drug sergeant, asking for help. Still there were no solutions. In cycling back and forth, I finally realized there really were no solutions. Imagine having a problem that is controlling your entire life, and then having no viable solutions to fix it. I had done everything within my power to stop this cycle and this behaviour and it literally stopped nothing. Even though I had given every ounce of effort possible, the issues only escalated. I realized that I had to stop owning the behaviours of everyone else. Those choices were not mine to own anymore. It really came down to that simple statement. *Owning what was mine to own.*

I was tired of feeling so full of shame and alone. Tired of feeling broken. Half the time I felt like I was losing my mind. I was tired of believing that this was my fault. I was in a cycle of shame, embarrassment and I felt like I was going crazy. I was tired of being at the end of my rope. It was time for me to be clear on what I wanted for my life. It was time to become more assertive and consistent with the direction I was choosing for my life. I deserved more than where my life was at in this chaos. Actually, we all deserved more.

> *"Your core values are the deeply held beliefs that authentically describe your soul."*
>
> **John C. Maxwell**

In 2009, I attended a leadership event and one of our main tasks for the weekend was defining our personal core values. After much deliberation, I was able to determine my values. From that point forward, my values became the basis for any decision in my life.

My core values were health, faith, family, fun, integrity, fulfillment, and commitment. My core values were the deciding factor for most of my decisions.

Two years into our story, I decided to look at my core values. I honestly forgot all about my core values and how I used them to make decisions in my life. I realized I wasn't living any of those values. Honestly, I was miserable on all levels. It had affected every single aspect of my life and it was starting to affect my personal health. I had to start to put some boundaries in place to save myself. There was no way I was going to survive in this environment without changing something.

I decided to do this for me and also for my boys. I didn't want my boys growing up believing that they could do whatever they wanted. At this point their current behaviour wouldn't "fit into" normal society. Not even close – yet that was the message that society was sending back to them. They weren't going to school, they weren't coming home and money was always missing. They would be missing for days to weeks at a time, their drug use was rampant and it was affecting every single aspect of their lives. According to society, the police and the legal system, there was nothing wrong with what they were doing, because they were under the age of 16. Society took the young offenders act and swung the pendulum all the way to the other end. Kids facing legal consequences as minors were learning nothing, it truly was a joke for them, and then when they turned 18 and became adults, everything changed. We weren't setting them up for success at all because there were minimal consequences for their actions. This is from our experience and from watching and attending over 20 court dates in a matter of a few years. It was truly mind blowing to watch! This became a real turning point for the importance of respecting my boundaries.

The convictions of my personal boundaries were frequently tested. At one point, we had to press charges on both of our boys. In fact, we had to do it a number of times. There were no other possibilities anymore and no other choices. We were worried that if we didn't do so that we were going to completely lose one or both of our boys. In Canada, if something happens in the home, the adult is required to press the charges against the youth. Even if you are being threatened, or if there is property damage in your home, the police do not press charges. The parents are expected to do this. Not only were we fighting the world, the message was that we were the only ones who had a problem with what was happening.

As difficult as this time was, ironically, I felt clear and strong in my decisions. After that day, years later, my son asked me if I had it to do all over again, would I still charge him? I answered with a resounding Yes. I asked him if he was ever going to stop, and he said, "probably not". In fact, looking back, I would have pressed charges sooner. I do believe that it had to come to that point, to that horrible moment in time when the decision would dictate in which direction our life would proceed. It was an incredibly poignant fork in the road. That is the knowledge of my hindsight which is truly 20/20.

If I could go back in time, I would pass along this simple message to my younger self. This message I would read and recite frequently to help me with my daily roadblocks.

"You didn't start this. You didn't create this. You didn't bring this into your home. This is not your fault. You know what your values are. You know what values you wanted to teach your kids, and you need to stick to what you know. Trust yourself. Believe in yourself. Listen to yourself because you truly do have the answers. Don't worry about what everyone is thinking, or saying, or believing about you because it doesn't matter. You live in it, you're surrounded by it all the time, and you know what to do. This is not the easy road, this is what it truly means to be a parent. You are parenting your ass off and you know you have given it everything possible. You're doing what's necessary to help their future self have a chance for survival."

Boundaries:

"I allow myself to set healthy boundaries. To say no to what does not align with my values, to say yes to what does. Boundaries assist me to remain healthy, honest and living a life that is true to me."

Lee Horbachewski

Chapter Three

Rebuilding Me Again

"Almost every successful person begins with two beliefs: the future can be better than the present, and I have the power to make it so."

David Brooks

Our life didn't always look like this current picture of chaos. If you had told me that this would one day be our life, I would have said it's not possible. I never saw this coming. It definitely wasn't on the radar.

I believe that we must take responsibility for ourselves. It's likely because of my experience as a kinesiologist and working with everyone from athletes, to kids, to post rehab and post surgical clients. The results a client would achieve were because of the work and ownership that they took for themselves. I've always believed that we take responsibility for our own decisions, our actions, and as a result we choose what we do in our life. We learn how to make those choices by believing that we are capable and that we have the ability to create whatever life we want.

This was my simple mindset before drugs took over our lives. It changed drastically over these first few years.

I've always been a person who was fairly confident in my decisions – I was comfortable with being me. It didn't bother me if others didn't agree with me, and I never expected others to fully understand it. I was very driven and persistent. I was full of integrity and very loyal. Honestly I loved those traits. They had served me well in my life up until this point. When drugs entered our life, I became a very small person. I shrunk down. I went into hiding mode. I questioned every single thing I did or didn't do. I stopped trusting myself, stopped believing in myself, and I stopped taking care of myself. I lost myself completely. I hated where I was at in my life and, in fact, I hated myself. I didn't even recognize that this was my life anymore. I couldn't figure out where I had signed up for this mess.

I had to go back to basics if I was going to survive. Deep down, I believed that I was a caring person who enjoyed empowering others to take responsibility for their lives. That motto wasn't working for my kids, so I decided it was time to take and listen to my own advice. I reminded myself that I could choose to focus on everything that was going wrong in my life, or I could find a way to take responsibility for myself and shift my mindset.

Whenever I felt my mindset sway, I would put the positive back in. That would mean reading, listening to podcasts, writing, watching YouTube videos, whatever it took to bring my positive mindset back. Sometimes I was doing this multiple times an hour. I purposely surrounded myself with people that would help me to see through the muck, and people who would help me find the positive in life again. My real world was ugly at this time. I decided to do whatever I had to do to bring my mind back to the optimistic thoughts, to find something positive to grab and hold onto.

Counselling became an integral point in my life for me at this time. It really helped me to push away all the confusing emotions and get right down to the basics. I had to simplify my thoughts and ultimately my life. I could see glimpses of my life prior to this, and understand that I was still in there somewhere. I was building tiny moments of belief in myself that I could still find my way through this mess. I had no idea how and truthfully the HOW didn't matter. That's what I had to let go of. The HOW didn't matter at all, and the HOW would present itself when I started moving. The HOW would never find me if I simply stood still like the victim that I allowed myself to become. I had moments of faith that somehow, some way, I was going to get through this. I knew my own mindset, my own thoughts were controlling my mood, energy and outlook. Trying to be positive and practicing gratitude in this chaos seemed like an impossible task, yet I knew it was where I had to start.

"Your worst enemy cannot harm you as much as your own unguarded thoughts"

Buddha

Words, affirmations, and my habits affecting my mindset were the only things I could control. I would speak positive words daily. I would write them, speak them, post them throughout my house. When I was stuck in a negative mindset, I learned to shift it in the moment. When I had to make any decisions, I would ask myself, "Is this in line with my core values?" and over time I knew the answer within seconds. Sometimes the answer was, "No... you know what to do." I was having reflective conversations with myself all day long. It was a matter of taking many baby steps, constantly asking myself the questions, and honouring my answers. Eventually I learned to trust myself on a daily basis. That inner voice became stronger and louder. I was finding clarity – sometimes in a split second. I realized how small I was playing in my life, and by living the way I was I wasn't helping myself and I wasn't helping either of my boys.

I viewed personal mindset as something that became very critical during this whole process. It was something that I was learning that I could change on my own in the moment. Whether it was how I choose to handle a situation or how to choose my thoughts. If I continued to put good information in consistently throughout the day, then I could shift my mindset when it needed changing. It became such a strict practice when I was having a really bad moment or day that I could stop, change my words and almost instantly shift my mindset.

From the outside it looked easy. It looked like I had life all under control, and that I was so positive. What no one ever saw from behind the scenes was the consistent work that I put into improving this skill. It was a daily practice that I chose because I didn't want to live the way I was living. It honestly became that simple. I wanted something different for my life.

I stumbled onto these simple daily practices that were making a huge difference in my life. My awareness of my mindset was absolutely critical. I had to come face to face with where I was at, how low I was in my life, where my mindset was and how I wasn't the person that I knew. I wasn't being me any longer. I had truly lost myself and everything I knew about who I was had changed. Awareness was the first step before I could change anything. I knew before anything could change I had to be honest and aware of what I was thinking, doing and saying.

When I found myself starting with negative self-talk, a trick that I learned was to write it down or to say the words out loud. It was the fastest way to change my thoughts because I realized that there was no one in my life that I would let talk to me the way that I was talking to myself. This simple game I played with myself became a critical tool to shift my mindset in the moment. It also became the window for my understanding of judgment. Judgment of myself and judgment from others. This became a game changer in my life and I will cover it more in the next chapter.

I learned to change my mindset because I was missing the positive things in my life. This practice became about survival, and I had to change drastically if I was going to survive! I was working with clients, and faking it all day long. Then I would fake it on weekends, and pretend I was happy and that things were normal. I was wasting extreme amounts of energy. Energy that I didn't have at all. My cup was bone dry.

I quickly learned that if I could put some good information in and if I could read a little, listen to an audiobook or a podcast, I could listen to positive videos, I felt my energy level shift even an inch. Ultimately what I was learning was how to change my state. When it shifted, I felt like I had hope. I had a glimpse of belief that I could do this. I could live this life and hopefully survive. Sometimes I would have to repeat those tasks and tricks that worked for me multiple times an hour and sometimes all day long. This wasn't the best long-term solution, yet I was learning in stages. We never learn it all at once. It is always one step at a time.

> *"You are the average of the five people you spend the most time with."*
>
> *Jim Rohn*

As I was building my positive belief system, I started to embrace the term "inner circle". My husband and I were becoming more and more isolated from others. Wherever we went, people would look, point, ask questions, or avoid us as if they hadn't seen us in the first place. The stress was unbearable. Going for groceries became a nightmare. I would go out at odd times, doing my best to avoid people. I felt like we must have had the plague by the way some people would look at and talk to us. My interpretation from most people's reactions was that it was all our fault and why did we not do something as parents to fix what was happening in our family. I am not sure who was more uncomfortable, I just know that seeing anyone else was beyond stressful. I simply wanted to live in a bubble to be safe, but of course that isn't the definition of safety. It was a very false sense of security, and it definitely wasn't a way to live. It was a very short term bandaid on a massive gaping wound.

My definition of inner circle was the group of people who I could spend time with that would not take energy away from me to be around them. My energy levels were incredibly low, I didn't have a lot of strength at that point in my life. I quickly learned that I had to be selective of who I spent my time with. My inner circle was changing constantly and I reminded myself that it was an "Invite Only" space. No one got a free pass. I had to be that selective if I was going to survive. I decided on a moment-by-moment basis who was in that circle and who was not. My inner circle completely transformed over this time period, and in hindsight I couldn't be more grateful.

I knew if I was putting positive information into my brain, for example the books, podcasts and videos, the exact same principle applied to people. I chose to surround myself with people who made me feel the same way. Even to this day, I still make the same choices. I literally chose to surround myself with people who could feed me positively, to help me to stay strong, and who believed in me. That was another shift that helped me to focus on the positive, and truly survive another day. If a person was negative, living in judgment, or took energy from me, they weren't in my inner circle. I had no extra energy to spare.

This process became a way for me to safeguard and protect my energy with the hopes of continuing to build my energy, my self-esteem and my confidence. When I listened to my intuition, it always guided me to who I should spend more time with and who I should limit my time with. I would reiterate that this was not out of anger, frustration or resentment. It was simply a choice. This became the beginning of me choosing what was best for me in order to survive. Survival truly became my daily goal. I had to learn how to survive before I could figure out how to thrive in my life.

Family or my friends at the time did not get a pass to be in my circle. That was a very difficult one for some people to understand. Some people struggled with this because as they were learning to process what was going on they would ask a lot of questions. When they asked questions, I would perceive it as being judgmental; maybe it wasn't at all, yet that's where my perception was at this point in time. I was not in a very stable space and I was learning to listen to what I needed to survive one more day.

My inner circle changed so much during this experience. In fact, it drastically changed, and in some instances it did a complete 360 degrees transformation. Some of my closest friends I had going into that period of time I don't even speak to anymore. They either stopped returning calls or they completely disappeared. In the beginning I was confused and didn't know how to handle this added stress. As time passed, I let go of my anger and frustration for two reasons. First, it became too much to carry and process and that alone was exhausting. Secondly, it was a much bigger issue than some people knew how to handle. I had to grow as a person to learn how to handle this mess and I couldn't expect other people to know how to handle it. They weren't living it.

Ironically when a few people left my life, it created space. Space I truly needed to have for the incredible new friends and people who came into my life. To this day, one of my closest friends is someone I have only known for a few years and only because of our similarities in our stories. Creating space is simply that: space.

I learned to create space where I needed it and to honour and respect that some days I simply needed more space. The more I listened to what I needed, the more I valued myself. The more I valued myself the more I listened to what I needed. It became a positive circle and for once I was finding a way to be in a positive spiral.

As I started to honour and listen to my inner voice and respect my values, I noticed that my mindset would improve. A positive mindset then improved my personal belief system, which improved my mindset and energy. I started to feel like the person that I was long before this ever happened, a new and improved version. I had completely lost myself in this process. The biggest gift was that I actually started to find myself again.

"Your beliefs become your thoughts,
Your thoughts become your words,
Your words become your actions,
Your actions become your habits,
Your habits become your values
Your values become your destiny."

Mahatma Gandhi

These daily habits became my lifeline. I started my morning with some form of exercise, either a run or a walk. I would listen to a podcast that was positive and would feed my mindset. I would spend 10 - 15 minutes writing and reading affirmations. Self guided meditations would give me time to focus on breathing and calm down my spinning mind. They became part of my reset button, and that button required resetting multiple times a day. Some days I needed multiple exercise breaks during the day. I also started hot yoga. Yoga helped me to live in the present. The past was suffocating and I spent hours reliving the circumstances, constantly doubting every single decision we did or did not make. The future was something I dreaded because I didn't know if my boys would survive. I didn't know where to live, and my thoughts wouldn't stop spiralling. I could only live in the present moment as it was the only moment I truly had. That is what I learned from yoga and the lessons were invaluable. To this day, I am beyond grateful for my regular hot yoga practice and for the people I surrounded myself with in yoga. It had more impact on my life than they will ever know.

I now realize that I am a recovering perfectionist. This personality trait did not serve me in this chaos. I have learned to keep my emotions checked in and grounded. When my emotions are out of control, my energy plummets. There were days where this would happen and I would allow myself the time and space to be low on energy. I learned to set up a mental timer, and after X amount of time, I would convince myself to change my environment, change my state, get active, go to yoga, go for a walk etc. Anything that would change my state. Changing my state would bring my energy back again. I became very aware when my emotions were low and typically it was because I had neglected my non-negotiables such as my reading, writing, meditation, or exercising.

I learned to listen to and honour what I needed and not judge it. There were some days that I really needed to spend time by myself and there were some days I really needed to spend time with friends. If I needed fresh air and sunshine I went out and got it. If I needed yoga I went and did it. I learned to honour and listen to what my body needed that day. Some days I could wake up and have the energy to take on the world and other times it would take me days to come down from the chaos. I learned to give myself time and space and to not judge what I needed at that moment in time. I learned the importance of self-compassion. This experience was changing me on levels I could have never predicted. In the past, I was a push person, one who never quit anything. I learned self-compassion because without it, I wouldn't have survived.

Chapter Four

<u>Building My Tribe</u>

"There's no need to be perfect to inspire others. Let people get inspired by how you deal with your imperfections."

Brene Brown

The term tribe to me means "my people". Who do I call when I'm in a pinch? Who do I reach out to when I need support? Who comes to mind first? Who do I like to spend my time with?

Understanding my personal core values made it even easier to find my tribe. Again, my tribe changed so much during these years. Integrity was definitely my top core value at this time. People who were very loyal, true to themselves, and authentic, were my favourite people. I surrounded myself with people with these traits. They were honest, supportive, and non-judgmental. They continued to help me fill my cup and keep me strong. When I was having those moments when I didn't trust myself and I wasn't sure which direction to go, I usually had a handful of people in my inner circle that I could call. They were completely invaluable, and to this day I am forever grateful for the role they played and continue to play in my life.

I became clear and honest about who I wanted to spend my time with. If I was spending a lot of time and energy around the wrong people I would end up feeling drained and exhausted. I had very limited resources and I struggled with recharging myself. I decided that if people weren't fitting in those criteria that they would not be part of my current inner circle. If a person was making negative or judgmental comments, or being critical of others, it was a light bulb that said, "I can't be around that right now." I learned to protect my energy as if it was gold because it was gold. It was helping me to survive.

There were a few people that I shared my story with that had been long time friends and I don't see them anymore. I was very vulnerable, and shared my story because I didn't know who to go to so I spoke to the people that I was the closest to at that point in time. In some of those cases, our situation became part of a gossip story that was shared far more than I expected. In hindsight, I wish I didn't initially share it with them, yet I do understand that it was all part of the growth I had to experience. I learned to let it go and not take it personally. Truthfully, none of us knew what to do or how to handle this situation. There was no manual for any of us to use.

I started to embrace being vulnerable because in being vulnerable I actually met some of the most amazing people who are now a major part of my inner circle. I couldn't imagine them not being in my life. One night I was on Facebook and I saw a post from someone I vaguely knew from a distance. I read between the lines in her post and her story sounded far too familiar. I sent her a private message; we connected shortly after that, we talked for hours and we have been close friends ever since. To this day I am grateful that she was vulnerable enough to share her story, and that I was vulnerable enough to reach out and send her a message. By allowing myself to be vulnerable, it brought some of the most incredible people into my life. People who helped me to get through one more day. Life was slowly becoming about more than simply surviving.

> *"Vulnerability is not winning or losing; it's having the courage to show up and be seen when we have no control over the outcome. Vulnerability is not weakness; it's our greatest measure of courage."*
>
> **Brene Brown**

In the first few years of dealing with drug use and our kids, I spent a lot of time stuck in the fear of judgment of others. I let this fear dictate whether or not I would reach out to connect with other people. One night I had this incredible ah-ha moment when I realized that there was no one who could judge me harder than I had judged myself. I spent two years completely tearing myself down, belittling myself, assuming this was my fault, trying to own choices that weren't mine, trying to fix it, taking 100% of the blame for what had happened to our family. I approached everything in my life with hurt and anger because I was filled with hurt and anger. This was such a pivotal moment in my life because I finally realized that it wasn't mine to own anymore. I finally had my first experience of letting go and surrendering.

This experience of vulnerability and surrendering correlated with a growth in my strength and courage. A friend introduced me to Brene Brown's Ted Talk on Vulnerability and her books and it was perfect timing. I learned that being vulnerable was where I found my courage. I allowed myself to be vulnerable, to stand in my own integrity, to be authentic, and the more I did that, the more courage I gained. The more courage I gained, the more vulnerable I became. This cycle was a true shift in my personal power. When I embraced the notion that no one could judge me harder than I had judged myself, I released the judgment piece. I simply let it go. It was something that held me down and kept me stuck for a long time. Learning to let go was an incredibly freeing experience.

The more vulnerable I became, the more I met incredible people who impacted my life in such simple ways.

This continued to encourage and support me more than I anticipated on a day-to-day basis. The more vulnerable I became, the more I felt like I was gaining my power again. I felt like I was finally living in integrity and being authentic with the world. The more I shared my story, the more free I felt and the more my courage grew.

It became even easier to let go of judgment because it really wasn't part of the equation anymore. Fear of judgment of others kept me a prisoner for many years and all of the sudden it was barely an issue. It was such a strange twist of fate and energy for me and I was so grateful for learning how to let go of the hold that judgment had in my life. I had let it rule my life for years. I truly understood that vulnerability wasn't a sign of weakness….in fact I believed it was a sign of strength, and I was starting to feel stronger every single day.

This experience unleashed something within my soul. The more I spoke to others, the more I understood the magnitude of this problem and how many families it was impacting. I met parents hiding in shame, not living in their current lives. The more people I connected with, the more my courage grew. My courage grew from my speaking to others, writing blog posts, writing Facebook posts, recording videos and generally connecting with others who needed support. I spent years feeling so powerless and helpless and for the first time I understood that I wasn't powerless at all. No one could take my power away. The only way I lost it is if I gave it away, and I was tired of giving it away.

Being vulnerable with others shifted the power in my life back to me. It didn't change our situation, and it didn't change my boys. It simply restored my personal power. This was the power in allowing me to be myself and the power of believing in myself again.

> *"People come into your life for a reason, a season or a lifetime. Think about the people in your life over the years. Whether they were there for a reason, a season or a lifetime, accept them and treasure them for however long they were meant to be a part of your life. And when they are gone, be thankful for the gifts you received from them when they were here — for a reason, a season or a lifetime."*
>
> *Unknown*

I am happily surprised in my current tribe because there's new people that I didn't even know before this ever happened. There are people that I thought would be there that have disappeared. I learned to let that go. I don't hold any anger with that any longer because it's too heavy of a weight to bear and it's not necessary to carry this load. It's not even mine to carry.

Who is in my tribe is who is meant to be in that tribe. It's that simple. To this day, that is one of my top gratitudes every single day. This tribe of superstars are the friends that keep me anchored and give me strength, spirit and hope again. They pour their belief into me when I need it and I borrow their strength and belief when mine is low. They remind me of the importance of having fun in life, because fun was on the back burner for so many years. I am forever grateful for my tribe.

My tribe became a massive part of my personal growth. I wasted so much energy being angry about who was and who wasn't there, because I felt so alone. The anger piece took a long time to work through. I finally learned that my thoughts and feelings were my choice and if I didn't like them, I could choose different thoughts and feelings. It may sound silly, but it truly became that simple. If I really peeled it back and dissected the feelings, it was more about the sadness that our family experienced and what we lost.

My tribe reminds me to stay in the present. They are a critical part of my strength, my main anchor. Most days my tribe might be a handful of people and that is plenty. They are truly a massive reason as to why I am still standing today.

In the past when I would reach out to a friend to talk, it became a session to complain and not truly looking for a solution. This situation was different. In a time of crisis, it's important to reach out to others who are a sounding board, friends who can help to ground you when you're stuck and overwhelmed. In those critical moments, experiences that I couldn't do justice to describe, I needed friends who would remind me to slow down, stay in the present and stop the spiral. That is the role my current tribe plays in my life and it is vital to who I am today.

As a parent dealing with teen substance abuse at the level that we were experiencing, a tribe is important, critical and necessary. In our particular situation, most parents spend their time alone, living in shame, and hiding their story and their pain and suffering from the world. We isolate ourselves to protect ourselves and our families, but it truly is a bandaid, and not a good one at that! This beast cannot be tackled alone. Parents need a tribe as a sounding board, a rock to help build their courage and strength again. That is the only way a parent can move forward, because it will never ever happen alone.

> *"When we find the courage to share our experiences and the compassion to hear others tell their stories, we force shame out of hiding and end the silence."*
>
> *Brene Brown*

Chapter Five

Facing My Fears and
Finding My Courage

"God grant me the serenity to accept the things I cannot change; the courage to change the things I can; and the wisdom to know the difference."

Serenity Prayer

From the very first time we found drugs in our home, one of my greatest fears was that people would find out. What would they think? What would they think of me? What would they think of my kids? What would they say about us as parents?

Some of my fears were not real. My thoughts were caught up in my perception of what other people would think. My fears kept me very stuck, paranoid, in hiding, and pretending that everything was perfect. My initial fears were irrational, as most fears typically are. After those initial thoughts, my next fears were focused on what to do to stop the drugs in our home. No matter what we tried it never stopped, and it never went away. Drugs were present in our home more often than I could track. For many months we didn't know what would happen in our home on any given day. It could be the calmest, quietest day that erupted into an explosive situation and something being broken or damaged. We lived on eggshells daily —our boys not coming home for hours or days, we had no idea where they were, and daily phone calls from the schools. Life was ridiculously unpredictable. I lived in a state of constant fear that showed no signs of letting up, or stopping.

This state of fear created such a toxic energy that infected all of our lives, including our marriage. At this point, Brad and I had been married for 22 years. We had a very loving, supportive marriage. We were very blessed. The presence of drugs in our home was certainly challenging our marriage, as it was affecting every piece of our lives. There were times we couldn't even leave our house, not for a dinner, a movie or a coffee. Typically when we left our home to get out, we would come home to absolute chaos. At one point we decided that we needed to get out for a dinner for our anniversary, and in 2 short hours we came home to extra kids in our home, with alcohol and drugs present. We didn't want to be home and we couldn't get away from it. We hid from the world and we hid from each other. We were in so much pain. Pain in our thoughts, pain for no solutions and pain because we were so afraid of what the future held for our boys. The more we hid from the world and from each other, the further we pulled apart. We were lost because we had no idea what to do anymore. There was no happiness, no joy, no space and definitely no life. Our existence was becoming smaller and smaller. We lost ourselves during this time, individually and as a couple. It was truly a heart-wrenching experience.

Even though most of my fears were focused around the things I couldn't control, they were physically holding me back from living in my life. Being stuck for the first 2 years was the norm because I wasn't ready to rationally deal with my thoughts and fears. Once I started to reach out, find my tribe, be honest, listen to my values, and what I wanted with my life, only then could I start to take baby steps in moving forward. I had to learn to own what was mine and that included my choices, my actions, my reactions, my attitude and behaviours. It was such a steep learning curve to own what was mine and let go of everything else. I spent so much time worried about all of the things I couldn't control and next to no energy on the things that I could control. As I made this transition to understanding my fears and letting go of control, I understood that most of my fears were about things that I had zero control over. When I could reason through those fears, I then had to come to grips with my fears about the future for my kids. At this point of our story, I had no idea what was going to happen with my kids. I had visions of losing one or both of our boys, either by suicide, overdose or potentially incarceration. These weren't unfounded fears. Yet they were still fears that I couldn't fix or control.

It took me a long time to fully understand and deal with these emotions and fears. I vividly remember sitting on the floor in a corner, curled up in a ball, crying hysterically and wondering how this was my life? I screamed, I yelled and I felt broken. I was angry at the world, hating my life and hating that I was in this same moment again, day after day. Hate was an emotion that was consuming all aspects of my life.

Sorting through the fears and emotions took a physical toll on my body. I experienced all of the emotions from extreme fatigue, headaches/migraines, exhaustion and an achy sense of pain throughout my body. I was so weighed down with emotions, as though I was an anchor stuck at the bottom of the ocean. I couldn't move and I didn't want to move anymore. I honestly wanted to die. The pain was unbearable and there was no end in sight, only escalation. It was as though my fears had a physical hold on me, holding me down, suffocating me and preventing me from living my life.

Over time I finally realized that I was the one holding onto those fears and if I wanted change I simply had to let them go and surrender. This lesson was pivotal in my survival.

There was one specific low moment when I swear I heard a voice that said, "You have a choice." I didn't understand. Then it hit me, if they could choose to use drugs and choose how they lived their life, then I could also choose how I lived my life. I could choose how I lived and in what conditions I lived. The word *choice* became the word that literally helped me to overcome a lot of my fears, simply because I finally decided to own my own right to choose.

Chapter Six

The Two S's — Self Compassion and Surrendering

"Self-compassion is key because when we're able to be gentle with ourselves in the midst of shame, we're more likely to reach out, connect and experience empathy."

Brene Brown

Being a compassionate person was always an important priority to me. Helping others, being aware of others' feelings and caring about the wellbeing of others likely led me into the field of health and wellness. I truly aspired to make a difference in the lives of others.

It wasn't until a close friend from my tribe reminded me that I wasn't showing a fraction of that compassion toward myself that the word self-compassion hit home. That's when I realized that how I show love toward others and how I care for others is going to stem directly from how I take care of and how I feel about myself. Compassion starts inside with us and this was a massive light bulb moment. I learned to give myself space when I needed it and to have a low moment without judgment. I really had to learn self-compassion the hard way, when I was the most broken. That had to come first.

This skill was not an easy lesson to learn. I still felt responsible for the demise of our family. It may not seem logical or make any sense but internally I believed that a parent was supposed to be able to fix everything. That was the ridiculous message I continuously repeated on an internal level and the standard that I held over myself.

As a working mom, running a business, with kids that were always busy with sports and activities, it felt like I was always trying to do it all. I was trying to live up to this ridiculous definition that I believed I was supposed to achieve. I know I was not alone in striving for this level of perfection. It was completely unattainable. We, as moms, put ourselves on the back burner. I put myself so far on the back burner that I don't even think I was even on the stove anymore. I had to learn to be very honest and compassionate with what I needed. My husband was very good at that. He reminded me to go to yoga, to go for a run and to take time for myself. I am grateful for that, because this was not an easy adaptation for me to learn.

These lessons became easier when I embraced the power of surrendering. That was a word that I struggled with because it felt like I was giving up or quitting, and I was not a quitter. I didn't put a lot of time or emphasis into surrendering until it was the last step to learn. Ironically, it's the one word that was critical for me moving forward in my life and it was the step that I resisted the most.

In owning my own story, I began to understand what parts of the story were mine to own. Anything that I couldn't control, couldn't change or fix wasn't mine to control, and those were the pieces that I had to release. In essence I surrendered those pieces of my story. I stopped taking responsibility for decisions that I wasn't making. This step-by-step process allowed me to see that the only thing I could control was me...my decisions, my choices, my actions, and my reactions. That's it! I came to terms with the fact that I'd done everything that I could with my boys, and it still didn't matter. It didn't stop, change or fix their behaviour. Instead it escalated. They were still going to do what they wanted to do. If it wasn't mine to own, then it wasn't mine to fix anymore.

During these years and to this day the word surrender meant everything to me. So much so that I wore the serenity prayer on my wrist. I found it in a bracelet and I read it over, and over, and over again, all day long. It became a corner-stone for me and a very monumental word in my life. I needed to surround myself with constant reminders to surrender anything that wasn't mine to own.

To this day I still wear my bracelet daily. If I found myself stuck in a moment where my thoughts were, "I have to fix this, I have to change this, or I have to control this," I would stop and say the serenity prayer out loud. As soon as I said it out loud, I would realize that my thoughts were either irrational or they were non-serving and that's when I could almost shift my mindset in the moment. I learned that words inside my head were toxic, and when I said them out loud, they lost their power. Eventually I learned to shift my mindset almost like the snap of a finger. I would say, "No, that's not mine to own, that's not mine to fix, I must let that go." I would surrender in the moment. It became a practice I repeated all day long.

It may sound as though it was a simple thing to do. It wasn't at all. As time passed it became very clear from daily practice, and from saying it out loud, that surrendering was one of the main keys to changing my life. I had to take the thoughts from out of my head – every time I would think too much, or plan ahead, or worry, I would make myself say the thoughts out loud. As soon as I would say them out loud I realized I wouldn't talk to anyone that way and I wouldn't let anyone else talk to me that way. It made my thoughts a reality and that's how I could determine how much power to give them. Most of the time my thoughts were based on future events, worries and concerns that I couldn't control anyways. I verbally talked to myself out loud, daily, all day, as often as I needed to do in order to put my thoughts and my life into perspective.

Since I originally felt that surrendering was a sign of weakness, it took me a long time to embrace it. As a result of learning to let go, I was surprised to find a huge amount of inner peace. I never expected to find peace by letting go. It doesn't mean that I don't have sad moments and moments that aren't incredibly difficult. For the first time I was able to truly find a new level of peace. I missed having peace in my life, and I was learning that if I wanted it, that it had to start with me. I could create the peace I was desperately searching for.

Once I learned how to surrender and find inner peace, I felt like I could move and finally live again. Over time I felt that I could trust myself again. I felt that I could enjoy life, have happiness and be more of me. I felt like I had a chance at life again.

I wish I could have learned this lesson sooner. This is a lesson I could only learn by doing. I spent my life as a Type A person, who was driven by hard work. My interpretation of surrender was that it was giving up and not trying. It was the complete opposite. I was wrong, absolutely 100% wrong.

Our greatest strengths tend to become our biggest weaknesses. Persistence, dedication, pushing harder, those skills did not serve me when our family was affected by drug use. I had to learn new skills. I had to do the direct opposite. I wish that I could have learned to do this sooner but I believe I had to go through all those experiences before I could embrace the actions of surrendering.

Surrendering helped me to survive on a daily basis. It reminded me to get out of my overwhelmed brain and stay in the present moment. When I caught myself thinking in overwhelm and focusing on the future, I reminded myself to surrender and stay in the present moment. That is truly the only moment we have. It allowed me to focus back on what I can control and that was simply me.

The act of surrendering became something I practiced every single day. It literally became a cornerstone of my life. I learned to surrender the opinions of others, including friends and family. One of the toughest things to let go of was the fact that I had spent years creating and visualizing the picture of what life would look like, what our kids would achieve, and what they would accomplish.

I had to let go of all of those visions as those were made up stories because nobody would ask for this situation. I didn't ask for it, I didn't do anything wrong to deserve it. It just happened. It was just based on choices that I couldn't control. I had to really learn to let that go in order to find some peace. Living in that dream day in and day out kept me from focusing on my reality. As long as I wasn't living in the present moment, I didn't have to deal with the reality of our life. It was a short term band-aid that was preventing me from moving forward in my life. I had to get to the place where I didn't choose to be in that space any longer and I was finally connecting the dots.

I found myself constantly asking the question "Why?" Why is a victim's question and the victim question kept me stuck as a victim. It truly applies to everything in life. Why questions are redundant questions because there is no answer that could possibly justify the hell we were living in and that became a massive waste of energy. Precious energy that I didn't have any more. My cup wasn't low. It was bone dry.

Every time I caught myself asking a why question I would ask, "Why does it matter?", because the why no longer mattered. I changed my questions to WHAT questions. What is an action word and if I could mentally just switch in the moment and go into action mode, then I could do something with my situation. The word why literally became a negative word for me, a word I would stop myself from using. I physically removed it from my vocabulary. Once I heard my husband saying, "Why is this happening?" or "If we had done this differently then things would be different." My answer to him was, "Then go back and change that." Of course we couldn't, so letting go of that statement became the action step. My energy couldn't go to things that we couldn't change or fix.

Self-compassion led me to embracing the importance of surrendering to anything that wasn't mine to control. This truly was the tipping point for me to beginning to create a shift in my life. The act of surrender became a habit and I was finally on the path to regaining my life again.

Chapter Seven

Finding My Inner Lion

"You were given this life because you are strong enough to live it"

Unknown

I always believed that I was a strong person; for some reason it is what I always told myself. I was exposed to a number of challenges early in life, but I never considered myself a victim. I attribute who I am today to my experiences and all of the difficult decisions that I never truly felt ready to make, yet I did. When do we ever feel ready to make the hard decisions in life? I am who I am today because of everything that I have experienced. To be grateful for who I have become requires that I express gratitude for the good and the hard experiences that life presented to me. There are lessons everywhere if we choose to see them.

Unfortunately, the challenges of my journey began at the tender age of twelve when I was a victim of a sexual assault from a group of boys in my school. This horrific experience impacted me deeply and influenced me to take 100% responsibility for my life. I will never forget the day that I decided to tell my parents what had happened and we proceeded with dealing with the police. I couldn't bury it, God knows I tried. I was the only person who could put a stop to this, and that meant approaching my parents with what had happened and involving the police. This was a very big story in my small town and it required me to build an armour to protect and keep me safe from everyone else. That armour has been a blessing and a curse in my life. When I wear the armour to block out and protect myself from the negative things in life, I am also blocking the joy from coming in. That will still be one of my biggest ah-ha's in my life. I didn't need to carry and wear the armour 24/7 because I was missing the joy in my life. I grew up an entire lifetime during that experience. I found my courage and had to embrace and use it from a very young age.

Over the years I faced a number of challenges in my life: family, health, business, financial and personal. It felt like we were never on the easy path, if that even exists.

When drugs showed up in our life, I had no idea it was going to become the monster that it did. It was definitely our biggest life hurdle that we had to face with no warning. Drugs completely tore our family apart and took a piece of me with it. It was a demon and I was fighting something that was definitely more powerful than any of us. For the first few years, I went into hiding and I had no idea how to find my courage or even find that person that I knew I was underneath this mess.

When I started to slow down and really listen, honour myself, own my story, surround myself with my tribe, and start to feel more positive, then I felt that I could start to live my life again. I slowly started to build my courage. One decision, one experience and one step at a time. The more I listened and followed through, the more I learned to trust myself and my inner voice. It was a positive ripple effect that was ultimately re-building me in my life again.

We spend so much time looking for our courage. However, we actually have to be doing something, in action mode, making decisions to find our courage. We find it by falling down repeatedly, by making mistakes and by deciding what to do differently next time. It is a process that is always occurring. It is not a one time situation.

In my public speaking, I explain that life is like one big long hallway full of multiple doors. They represent different opportunities filled with twists and turns our life can take. We spend so much time in the hallway as we are afraid to open up a door because we don't know if it's the right door, or the perfect door, or what's there or what happens next. It is completely analysis paralysis. We do absolutely nothing except stare at the doors and overthink everything. We must accept that there is no perfect door, there is no perfect scenario, there is no ideal result because there's good and bad behind every single door that we open. We spend so much time looking at those doors because we can't find our courage to make a change in our life. We are too busy looking for our courage. We actually build our courage by opening up doors, by walking through them, making right choices, wrong choices and then building again. Courage is an action word, a verb. It is not a noun. We don't have courage, we build it. By consistently being in action mode, trying something, making mistakes, then making different choices, that is where we learn and build our courage.

When I started to trust myself to make decisions, my courage grew. I started to become the person that I felt I was before and a person that I was proud of. I felt that if I could find my courage then I could also help other people find their courage. It literally grew from there. I started to put myself out there in the public. I started sharing my lessons on social media. I started doing public speaking engagements. I stopped hiding and I started showing up. I started to live a more authentic life of integrity. While I was speaking at events, I realized how many others were suffering at the same time. I began to view my situation on a much larger global scale, and it put into perspective the amount of families that were suffering and hiding from the world. I knew I had to do something. I started believing that maybe this was the reason that our family went through this experience, because it was tied to something much larger than me. The more I thought about other people who were suffering, the more my courage continued to grow. It's not easy and it's definitely not perfect. I, like everyone else, am always a work in progress. I embrace being a work in progress as this is better than being stuck in a life and in a state that was suffocating.

> *"Have the courage to follow your heart and intuition. They somehow know what you truly want to become."*
>
> *Steve Jobs*

Chapter Eight

Building My Reserves — Let's Overflow That Cup

"Honour the physical temple that houses you by eating healthfully, exercising, listening to your body's needs, and treating it with dignity and love."

Dr. Wayne Dyer

Health:

For years one of my highest core values was integrity. When our life changed so drastically for the first 2-3 years of our journey, I wasn't living my life in integrity at all. In fact, it was the complete opposite. Whenever we live a life against our personal core values, that adds another layer of stress to an already stressful situation.

For 25 years I worked as a Kinesiologist and Personal Trainer. I coached and mentored people to make physical changes in their bodies and emotional transformations in their lives. I coached people to create substantial changes in their life.

In the early years of our chaos, I was completely out of integrity and alignment with who I was as a person. I had let my health go, I wasn't sleeping, and I wasn't taking care of myself. I was in a state of constant overwhelm and stress was at its peak point. My home life was the complete opposite of how I spent many years living and the polar opposite of how I was teaching my clients to live. I created change and improvement in the lives of others for a living. I felt like such a fraud in my own life.

This was one of the biggest wall kicking moments because I couldn't understand how I could be successful at work, yet I couldn't make that change in my home.

I took me time to realize the parallel that I did have a number of clients who didn't have great results in their programs. Maybe they weren't ready to make a change, or they didn't want to own their own decisions or choices, or they weren't open to listening to my coaching.

It was the same as at home. I couldn't own whether they were changing or successful or not because they weren't ready. I had to realize it wasn't because I was a success over here and a failure over there. It's the fact that if anyone wasn't ready to create a change then it wouldn't matter what words I used or how I coached them. They wouldn't see change or results. I couldn't own whether a client would be successful, ultimately it was up to them to do the work. This became the same lesson at home. In fact, it was the same lesson for creating change in my own life.

Exercise:

In order to survive I had to make some drastic changes. At this point my health had hit an all time low. I used to be an avid runner. I loved working out with weights, and fitness classes. I loved all different kinds of fitness. My health had always been a primary core value and a top priority for me. Truthfully I was feeling terrible at this point in my life. I had no energy, brutal sleeping habits, weight gain, headaches and migraines and I honestly felt like giving up on life. Before this time in my life, exercise was never about weight loss, body fat or clothing size. Exercise was always about managing my stress levels and helping me to sleep. It was the fact that I had to frequently remind myself that when I exercised I coped better, I slept better, I could think with more clarity and I felt in alignment. As a result, exercise took on very different roles at this point in my life.

Exercise became an absolutely critical part of how I dealt with my emotions on a day to day basis. I would remind myself, and still do, that when I exercise, I handle problems better, and I sleep better. When I finished exercising I would remind myself to remember how good I felt so that when tomorrow came and I didn't feel like exercising that it would be a reminder to fit it in no matter what. I would go through the process of convincing myself and reminding myself to do something every single day. If I wanted to be able to function in an incredibly chaotic, unpredictable environment, I had to start to find ways to take care of me. That became more than a priority, it became a necessity.

I remember being huddled on the floor in tears. I didn't think I could move. I was convinced that I was chained to the ground. I resented the world for our life, I hated that everyone else seemed happy and normal. I was equally mad for what I was doing to myself. I blamed the world and myself for where I was in my life. Blaming everyone still didn't change anything. I desperately wanted change and that meant that I had to do something drastically different from what I was doing. I was done being the living example of the definition of insanity.

Even though exercise had always been a huge part of my life, I had to change my forms of exercise because the old ways weren't working. For example, I was always a runner and loved lifting weights. Every time I pushed myself with either of these two activities, I was physically burnt out for days. Being burnt out was definitely not filling my cup. That's when I decided to look at different forms of exercise. The practice of hot yoga entered my life. I had tried yoga many times before and truthfully I never loved it. It felt slow, like I was not working hard enough and that I couldn't stay in the present moment (on my mat) without my head spiralling with everything that was wrong in my life. Again, what I was resisting was exactly what I needed to do. Yoga taught me how to breathe. It seemed ridiculous, but breathing was not something I focused on regularly. I breathed in a very shallow fashion, as a person who is living in high levels of anxiety does. I had to learn to slow down and learn to breathe. Breathing and concentrating on my breathing became an act that kept me in the present moment. I started practicing my breathing, being aware of my breathing and aware of what I was doing at the time. When I slowed my breathing down, and my thoughts came into the present moment, I started to feel a sense of calm and peace. Something as simple as breathing became one of my non-negotiables.

Non-Negotiables:

I started to look at the non-negotiables that I needed in life and decided to make a list of what needed changing. It was the basics: exercise, sleep, nutrition and meditation. I knew I had to come face-to-face and be aware of what I was doing to contribute to where I was at this point in life. Enough of the chips, wine, and comfort food. It wasn't comforting me or changing my situation. In fact, I think it kept me in the exact same space...stuck and feeling hopeless. I had to own my own actions and choices that brought me to that point in my life. I wasn't doing anything to take care of myself so it was ridiculous to be critical that I wasn't handling life well because I wasn't putting anything in the cup to refill it again. My cup was bone dry and it was up to me to fill my own cup. It was my cup after all, not anyone else's.

This is where the serenity prayer became a grounding practice for me. The only thing that I could truly control and take care of was myself. This was the epitome of the serenity prayer and it was time that I put this concept into practice in my own life.

This required me to be accountable to myself to fill my cup, and it also meant that I had to find some form of self-compassion at the same time. Some days I was at such a low point energy wise that I knew I needed to exercise but I had to recognize that I wasn't in the space to do a heavy weight workout or a long run. I learned to be forgiving of myself and simply ask my soul, "What do you need to do today?" Some days I needed to run, some days I needed to walk or do yoga. Either way I had to move in some way, shape or form. I just gave myself some leniency on what that movement would look like.

Once I recognized the importance of moving everyday, I then shifted from using exercise to punish myself to using exercise to fuel myself. I created the mantra that I required exercise to feed and fuel my body. Exercise served a purpose of giving me energy, giving me time for myself and as a by-product it was slowly building my reserves. Sometimes I needed a long power walk, time in some fresh air, and sometimes I needed the quiet present moment practice of yoga. Either way this put me into a form of action mode that I hadn't been in for a very long time. I learned to listen to what my body and mind needed that day and I would deliver what it needed. That also meant that I finally started to value what I needed, which led to me valuing myself again. I started to believe that I did matter.

The concept of filling my own cup first didn't register until I was at a leadership event in 2015. It was at this event in Las Vegas where I heard the famous speaker and coach Lisa Nichols speak, that I truly understood what this phrase meant. All day long, the challenges that we face in our life empty our cup. Life pulls from our cup, emptying it every single day. Even our daily responsibilities take from our cup. Our family was not living under normal daily conditions. Not even close to normal.

Lisa Nichols explained that the cup analogy was similar to the instructions we hear on the airplane to put our oxygen mask on first. We must fill our cup in order to be able to give to anyone else. Filling our cup requires putting regular deposits back into our cup every single day. Visualize holding a cup and a saucer. Our job is to fill the cup to the point of overflow and we serve others from the overflow. This hit home for me. There was no overflow in my cup, remember my cup was bone dry. I was responsible for filling my own cup. No one could fill it for me. Filling my cup meant being clear on my non-negotiables, and I identified them based on how I felt when I did certain activities. The things that made me feel better included reading, listening to podcasts or audiobooks, writing, exercise, good nutrition, committing to sleep, positive space for myself and especially staying in alignment with my own personal integrity.

Most people never fill their cup. They give and give and give until they feel so empty that they numb themselves with negative items such as food, alcohol, shopping or gambling. They also resent other people for not stepping up and helping them with their life, and that is not taking responsibility for their cup. I know because I did this for many years. I seriously lived with resentment for everyone who had what we didn't have. We all needed to learn how to fill our cup again.

I learned to be honest with myself by asking the hard questions. When my energy was low, I would ask myself, "What did I put into my cup today"? There were days that I had to be brutally honest with myself, and it was no coincidence that on my lowest days I wasn't putting anything into cup to refill it. One of my mantras was that, "my cup is a priority, and if I have to live in this chaos, I must fill my cup every single day." The refilling of my cup became a top priority in my daily life.

It wasn't long before I made the connection of filling my cup and building my gratitude practice.

Gratitude:

"Gratitude makes sense of our past, brings peace for today, and creates a vision for tomorrow."

Melody Beattie

When our family started to fall apart, gratitude seemed like a cruel joke. I struggled with being grateful because I believed I didn't have anything to be grateful for. I didn't ask for this life and I was stuck in the mindset of why us and thinking we must have done something wrong to deserve this. I made it all about me, as if life was happening TO me and not FOR me. I also resisted the word abundance because I certainly felt like we didn't live in abundance, as everything felt like a struggle. Even the word struggle was a word I had to strip from my language. This was a hopeless way to think and to live. I knew if I wanted to change where I was in my life, that I had to drastically change my daily habits.

Over time I learned to be grateful for what I had, no matter how small it seemed. It could be as simple as I went for a walk, I listened to a podcast, I felt a glimmer of strength. I truly learned to be grateful for the smallest things and surprisingly, my cup started to feel like it was filling up. At night I would write my 10 gratitudes a day or sometimes I would write two pages of gratitudes. I also recognized that when I was in the practice of gratitude that I felt my energy shift and change.

Every time I was in gratitude, I noticed that I felt better, as in stronger, lighter and less weighed down by the world. One of the things I was resisting the most was exactly what my body needed to do in order to handle what we had been given. Learning to be grateful also reminded me to live in the present moment and that was something I also resisted. My brain bounced back and forth from reliving the past and from fretting about the future. It wasn't easy to get my brain to live in the present moment. Yoga, meditation and gratitudes played a massive part in helping me to live in the present moment and ultimately shift my mindset.

> *"Gratitude turns what we have into enough, and more. It turns denial into acceptance, chaos into order, confusion into clarity...it makes sense of our past, brings peace for today, and creates a vision for tomorrow."*
>
> **Melody Beattie**

Nutrition:

"Eating well is a form of self-respect"
Unknown

Nutrition was always an incredibly important aspect of my life. I've always been very conscious of eating, what I ate and how I took care of myself. Approximately 15 years ago I went completely gluten and dairy free, not because it was the fad thing to do, it was long before that. I was sick for a number of years even as a child. I did not take my health lightly. Shortly before drugs entered our life, I started nutritional rebalancing and I found some superfood nutrition supplements that increased my energy and helped my body to deal with my high cortisol and stress levels. Making my nutrition a priority certainly helped me to feel stronger. When I felt stronger I made better choices. Anything to feel better, it made every single day a little bit easier. Even if my exercise was off, my nutrition was 90 per cent consistent, and that significantly affected my energy levels.

I was determined to create a list of non-negotiables that were positive vices instead of negative ones. I had a number of friends that wanted to go for drinks, to block it out, to bitch about life and I didn't want to go down that road. I didn't want to be the parent who turned to a substance to deal with my kids' substance abuse issues. In my life I felt it was a behaviour that was a complete oxymoron. I didn't want to need anything to fix where I was at in life. I wanted to be strong enough to handle where our life was at, and that required me to build my depleted reserves again. I was determined to use positive vices to help me through the day, and all I needed to do was make it through one day at a time, actually one moment at a time. I didn't have any major life goals during this time. I simply wanted to survive and grow stronger every single day.

Intuition:

"There is a voice that doesn't use words. Listen."
Rumi

I learned to listen to my intuition many years ago. If it wasn't for my intuition, I am truly not sure if I would even be alive today. When this chaos started, I completely stopped trusting myself and I didn't know how to find that inner trust again. I reminded myself of the earlier stories in my life where my intuition made a huge impact in my life, and ultimately saved my life.

There was one point where my health was in a serious state. At the age of 32 I had a miscarriage. I was not new to miscarriages. Prior to this I had 2 other miscarriages a few years earlier. This one was different. I was just under 20 weeks pregnant when I found out that I had a partial molar pregnancy. That is a pregnancy that started as a baby and then something went wrong and a mass grew on the baby, in which eventually the growth mass took over. During those first few months I had to wait for regular testing and results all while we had to plan for what to do if the biopsy came back as malignant. It was a whirlwind of stress and I had to find a way to live in the present moment, even though that present moment was terrifying. In the years that followed, I had 5 surgeries in 6 years, enduring levels of pain that at times were unbearable.

It was Christmas Eve of 2007 and I heard a voice that spoke and said if I didn't have a hysterectomy that this would be my last Christmas. Some may think that it's weird but it was a very real experience. Without a doubt, I knew that voice was real. After many appointments, and one more surgery, I had a hysterectomy at 38 years old. Before the surgery, the surgeon stated he would be leaving my ovaries because I was too young for a full hysterectomy. I disagreed and told him that my ovaries were a major part of the problem. I had zero doubts. After I came out of the anesthetic, the surgeon asked me, "How did you know?" As it turned out he said I probably wouldn't have seen 40, as that's how advanced the tumours were on my ovaries. The results came back and everything was benign, but I knew in my gut that something was seriously wrong with my current state of my health.

After this experience, I started to really listen to what I needed and didn't need. I truly started to trust my intuition. Ironically, if I hadn't had the partial molar pregnancy years earlier, I wouldn't have had the hysterectomy and who knows where I would be now. It was a clear experience of finding gratitude in a difficult situation. I learned to be thankful for the painful miscarriage and be grateful for the baby I lost that actually saved my life.

There was a complication post hysterectomy and a I had another surgery 18 months later. I then developed a staph infection from my hysterectomy that didn't present itself until almost one year later. I ended up being hospitalized for a few days with a Pic line and IV antibiotics for almost eight weeks. It was another surreal experience that was another threat to my health. I was scared and exhausted and desperately wanting to be healthy again. Unfortunately, it was during the time when drugs first entered our home. At least this is when we first found it. For a long time I thought, "OK, it's because I was sick, it's my health, it caused this, it caused that." etc.

It didn't cause the drugs, but it's where my head was for a long time. It is human nature to want to or need to blame someone for something. There was no blame here, just choices. My health has been challenged on a number of occasions and I've learned to value my health. My health is one of my daily gratitudes, that I am beyond grateful that my body is strong, and it allows me to function every day.

In the beginning stages I didn't exercise. I wasn't sleeping, or taking care of myself. I was gaining weight, losing muscle, and not feeling good about myself. It took going to that space to realize that I couldn't blame it on my circumstances and say my life was too chaotic, that I couldn't exercise or that I didn't have the time or any other excuse. I had to own what was mine and I had to choose to take care of myself again. I had to learn to make myself a priority in my own life. No one was going to do it for me. I slowly started to incorporate exercise into my weekly routine. I made a commitment to exercise at least 3-4 days per week and to never go more than 3 days without exercising.

It was ironic, making myself a priority was no longer a selfish act. It was a necessity. It was required. It was the only way I was going to survive. The more I focused on my health as a priority, the more I started to feel like I was in alignment with my personal integrity. I was on the path to finding myself, actually re-inventing myself.

Everything became a building block to rebuilding my health and my life again.

Even though these were all steps I went through, these steps truly intermeshed together. As I started to increase my energy, I started feeling more positive in my life. I wanted to exercise more because I had more energy. When I had more energy, I felt positive. I realized that all of those were pieces of the puzzle that really had to come together in order to help me to continue to move forward. All of the puzzle pieces were important and they had to exist together to build the puzzle. I was the puzzle. It wasn't about perfection. It was about listening to what my body needed in order to feed it, nourish it and take care of it. Slowly, one day, one action step after another, I started to feel stronger and believe that I could handle what we were given. None of this changed our situation with the boys, it simply changed how I handled the chaos in our lives.

Ironically I believe that making myself a priority and taking care of myself wasn't just helping me in my life. I believe that I am setting an example for my boys of what we all need to do to take care of ourselves.

If we want to change the situation that we're in then we first have to have awareness of the situation. We have to accept where we are at and that requires owning our own choices and our own actions. My boys will ultimately have to do the same thing, as will anyone else who wants to create a change in their life.

I will be there to support them at any point and time. As I've said to my boys, "I am not here to push or pull you through life. I can't fix your life for you. I am here to walk beside and support you while you create your own life." I believe if I do that with my own life, I'm setting an example and that they can do it as well.

These were all pieces of the puzzle: health, exercise, nutrition, non-negotiables, gratitude, and intuition. All of them were moving parts that all played a part in helping me to gain my strength, fill my cup to overflow and handle our life with grace and compassion.

Message to my younger self...

If I could go back in time and give my younger self a message I would simply say this...

> *"Trust yourself. You know what the answers are. You know what you need, what your body and mind need. Listen to the cues, trust yourself and follow through. You aren't here to fix everything, in fact you can only control yourself. Your actions, your reactions and your decisions are yours to own. When you exercise regularly and you take good care of yourself nutritionally you are going to be in a much better headspace to make decisions. You know what's important to you and you know what you need. You need to listen and respect yourself and be in integrity. You owe that to yourself and you deserve it. You need to do these activities in order to function. Trust yourself, you know the answers, you've always known the answers. Your voice matters."*

These lessons were incredibly important in becoming who I am today. People often say to me "You're very strong," as if being strong made sense for the challenges I was experiencing.

To some it appeared that I had everything in order, that I was positive and always able to handle the adversities our family was experiencing. I didn't just fall into this space, I crawled to get here. I crawled in the smallest baby steps, and I crawled through some of the ugliest and darkest days of my life. I was committed to my life. I wanted more for my life than where I was at. I worked through those lessons every single day in order to get to this point, the point where I could finally share my lessons with others. Even though those lessons were tied to some of the most painful experiences of my life, living through them was a critical experience and part of my survival.

> *"When you face difficult times, know that challenges are not sent to destroy you, they're sent to promote, increase and strengthen you."*
>
> ***Joel Osteen***

Chapter Nine

Finding The Gifts in My Adversity

"It is your reaction to adversity, not the adversity itself, that determines how your life's story will develop."

Dieter F. Uchtdorf

Gifts...

What a strange word to use for such an incredibly difficult experience.

I stumbled onto this word by accident. I started journaling and writing to sort through my thoughts. It took me so long to try to make sense of our life. Writing helped with the process. I was making progress and moving forward, yet a big part of me was still stuck.

I'm a very logical and analytical person, almost to a fault. I kept feeling as though there had to be a reason for why our family was in this experience. Every time I asked the question, I found myself stuck in the "why" question again and I knew that wasn't changing anything and it definitely wasn't productive. It was a constant game of tug of war. Then one day while I was writing, I realized that through this experience, I had finally found myself again. I found my strength, my voice, my courage, and my purpose. Ironically in the worst experience of my life is where I found myself again. I consciously started to call it a gift, because that would shift my anger and frustration. It would literally change my mindset and energy. If it truly was a gift, then I was meant to do something with it. It wasn't mine to keep to myself. It was mine to share with others, especially if I could use it to help others during the painful experiences in their life. The term gifts started to take on a life form of its own, and in that form it started to show me a much bigger picture which involved helping and impacting others.

Our gifts actually aren't for us. Our gifts are meant to be shared with and used to impact the lives of others. Paying it forward in some way, shape or form, became a new purpose. This was the birthplace of my speaking engagements and writing. It gave meaning to a much bigger purpose of what I was to do with our story.

> *"Something very beautiful happens to people when their world has fallen apart: a humility, a nobility, a higher intelligence emerges at just the point when our knees hit the floor."*
>
> *Marianne Williamson*

My Lessons Learned...

1. Most of my fears weren't real and they were definitely outside of my control. What was holding me back for the past few years were words inside of my head and the ridiculous yet initial constant fear of the judgment of others.

2. I have more strength than I realized.

3. I didn't live this life or endure this pain by accident.

4. I am here to be a messenger, to share with others who are stuck in their life. Being stuck does not have to be the norm.

5. I am not responsible for the decisions of others. That means I cannot take the blame for what others choose to do with their lives.

6. Our kids may be a reflection of us and the values that we worked hard to raise them with and instil in them. However, each person is born with their own brain and we each have the power to choose what to do with our lives in any given moment on any given day.

7. Life is too short to be living with fears, regret, sorrow and sadness. When I was experiencing these emotions, I was living in the past. The feelings of anxiety, fear and worry meant I was living in the future. Clarity is not available in either of those moments because those moments are full of what ifs, chaos and not living in the present moment. The present moment is truly the only moment that we have. I learned to

course correct as often as necessary, when my words were focusing on the past or the future. This is truly something that I currently commit to, and it is easier to course correct today because I have had a LOT of practice with this process.

8. I learned that there were people I could count on and others that I couldn't. I also learned the importance of counting on and trusting myself again. I can say this without any anger or frustration. That is too much effort to carry any more.It took an enormous amount of growth to get to this point in my life. Not everyone is willing to go through that growth because it's messy and usually downright ugly.

9. Forgiveness is necessary. The degree to which I can forgive others stems from my ability to forgive myself. In the beginning of this journey, I was consumed with anger, resentment and jealousy. Anger and hate are a ridiculously heavy load to carry, and I didn't realize the weight of that load until I set it down. I had to forgive myself for the break down in our family. I believed I failed everyone, myself, my boys and my husband. I learned to forgive myself for the unrealistic expectations I had and that helped me to forgive others as well. To everyone who walked away, avoided us and said hurtful things, I learned to forgive because everyone is speaking from their own position and I know my story stirred up a lot of fears in other parents as well. If it could happen to us, it could happen to their family as well.

10. Always choose love over fear. These are two opposing emotions and one cannot survive in the presence of the other, so always choose love.

11. Everyone is on their own journey, and when I let go of my expectations of others, and raised my own expectations of myself, that became a tremendous shift in my life.

12. Calling my experience a gift meant I was no longer a victim, and that was a massive change. Since I was no longer a victim, I could step into action mode. Victim and action are complete opposites and I was tired of being stuck. I chose not to live in chaos or as a victim any longer. More simply, I decided that was not how I was going to live my life.

The word gift completely shifted everything in my life.

I couldn't figure out how I could help others to understand that I chose to call it a gift, without everyone thinking I was crazy!

A friend and mentor asked me if I felt like I had made it through the darkest part of my journey? If I felt that I had made it to the other side? At this point in my life I honestly felt like I had shifted to a completely new space. My friend gently reminded me that since I felt as thought I had "made it through" the toughest parts of our story, that I had an obligation to share my lessons with others. I completely agreed.

This explains the analogy that I used to outline my journey, and I don't tend to sugar coat things.

"In life our adversities and our challenges are like a big pile of crap. Crap might sound like a harsh word, but it's a pile of all of the things we don't want to deal with. We avoid the tough stuff in life. We're stuck in our crap, we're stuck in our story, we're stuck in all of it because we are trying to remold it, reshape it, and make it look better. We even try to hide it and do everything except actually deal with it. In order to deal with it we have to dig through the trenches, we have to be willing to get dirty and messy. We have to be buried in it and at times we almost suffocate. We have to crawl our way through to get to the other side.

We must choose to do something different, if we want different results. We cannot stand outside the pile of crap, afraid to put our toe in it because it looks messy. We cannot avoid or resist it. We have to go through it. Whatever we resist, persists. We have to go through it to get to the other side. I was tired of the resisting and persisting cycle. It was time to create a more permanent change in my life."

Once we cross to the other side, the clarity is unreal. It's a completely different picture.

When I found my clarity, I literally stopped owning their decisions. The more I stopped owning their choices and decisions, and playing the blame game, the more everyone didn't know what to do with me or how to handle me. Honestly, I completely changed. My family and friends initially didn't know how react to the new me. During these shifts I felt I had regained my internal power which kept me motivated to keep going. I was controlling my own growth at this point. I was no longer reacting to life. I was directing it. What a massive shift in my own personal power! The more clarity I found the more I wanted to find. I was starting to live a life in alignment with my values for the first time years.

My boundaries became crystal clear. I knew where my boundary line was and when it had been crossed. As soon as it was crossed, I could confidently say, "Nope, this is my boundary line." It became that clear. That in and of itself became a huge gift in my life. It made all of my decisions easier to make as I knew my own values and what I wanted to do, who I wanted to surround myself with and what I wanted to expose myself to. Everything became easier and there was clarity everywhere.

Another mentor asked me if I was willing to share my journey with others. I hesitated as I couldn't imagine what others would think of me. Then I remembered that it wasn't about me anymore. It was about how I could pay it forward, to ease the journey for others. How could I use it to show others that they weren't alone?

For some reason this was our story, what mattered was what I decided to do with what we were given?

> *"At the end of life, what really matters is not what we bought but what we built; not what we got but what we shared; not our competence but our character; and not our success, but our significance. Live a life that matters. Live a life of love."*
>
> *Unknown*

During our journey, I had crossed paths with a number of people who were suffering in silence. I recognize that path because it was mine for years. That was a light switch moment for me. It just clicked. It became the start of me sharing my journey.

The other reason I decided to share my story was because it was clear that our family was only one of thousands of "good" families affected by teen substance abuse and addiction. I met people in person, at events, online and I knew that I was barely scratching the surface. It's a massive problem in society. The more I allowed myself to be vulnerable, the more I realized how many people this affected, and how many others were suffering in silence. I knew and believed with certainty that this was something that I had to share.

The more I shared it, the more my courage grew. I felt that much stronger, and became even more convicted in my words and my message. I was finally learning to trust myself again. In 2016, I gave a talk to an audience of 500 people. My husband and immediate family came to the event, and he said how proud he was and he understood why this was such an important mission for me.

I honestly feel that I have found my purpose. I believe that I am supposed to speak to people and help people release their shame. I am here to coach, support and mentor people who are stuck in their adversity. Their challenges may be very different than mine. Whatever the challenge, I learned that I am here to help people to find their voice, to break the pattern in their life, to live a life unstuck, and write a new ending to their story. In all of this chaos, craziness and mess, this was the one thing that I felt the most clear about. I didn't know what it was going to look like but I knew it was a path that I had to pursue. It was my path, purpose and journey rolled into one. Every time I share the story, I gain energy from it, I gain more clarity and courage and I keep moving forward.

Changing my words, and calling this a gift, helped me let go of my anger. It wasn't until I let go of my anger that I realized how heavy it was. It weighed a ton and I was physically and emotionally spent from carrying it for so many years. The anger was directed towards my boys and their choices, and to myself thinking I had to be responsible in some manner for where our life was at. I was also angry at the world because it felt like every other family had what I wanted for my family. Carrying anger was hurting me more than it was hurting anyone else. It wasn't changing the situation, and it wasn't helping my boys. It actually was a controlling piece for them. They could use that to manipulate me and it wasn't difficult since they were my kids. The emotional card was easy for them to use because I made it easy. I was too emotional and reacting to life and to everyone around me.

When I was in a heightened emotional state, when I was angry, I was responding with emotions and not with logic or reason. Once I shifted and let go of the anger, I found clarity. It was that simple. "These are the rules, you didn't follow them, you can't stay. You know what the rules are, they're not hidden, you can't stay because I respect what the rules are." I just learned to really trust myself. I was confident in who I was and who I was becoming, and that left little room for any manipulation or misdirection. I was living the mantra that we are all responsible for our choices in life.

This mindset was the beginning of us committing to and working on our marriage again. When we initially battled drugs in our home, we fought the battle individually. We were lost and losing hope every single day. In the beginning we were spending so much time blaming ourselves for where things were at. We were broken and we were in a spiral of desperately trying to fix everything. There was no happiness, no good memories and no joy. We stopped planning for our future, we stopped connecting and we went into robot mode. We avoided conversations because we were tired of talking about the chaos, and we were petrified about all of our futures. Those were some of our darkest days.

We didn't grow and change at the same speed. It wasn't a race, it just didn't initially happen together. In all honestly, I left home for a short period of time. I couldn't do it anymore. I resisted this because I felt like I was quitting and I was definitely not a quitter. Eventually I realized that I wasn't quitting. I was simply choosing me. I was choosing how I wanted to live and what I wanted for my life. We all get to choose.

When we finally realized how far apart we were growing we decided to truly work on our marriage together. We always said that if our kids came back to us that we wanted to be a springboard for them and not a pile of sand.

We really made a concerted effort. We got counselling and support from mentors in order to get the help we needed. We were also ready and open to receive the help.

Marriage is always a work in progress. The road to fixing our marriage started by taking care of ourselves individually. If we were both broken, we couldn't make "us" whole again. That's the piece a lot of people miss. When we're "off", most of the time we can attribute it to not taking care of ourselves individually.

It was time to put effort and emotions back into our marriage or that would be the next thing that we would lose. We spent five years trying to fix something that we had zero power in fixing. Once we realized that we couldn't own their choices and we could only take responsibility for ourselves, then we began to do the work to move forward.

Now we are definitely valuing our marriage and realizing the importance of each other. I feel as though we set an example for the boys and at one point in time they'll realize mom and dad didn't quit on each other either.

Chapter Ten

Grieving and Guilt — Let that sh&t go

"One of the hardest lessons in life is letting go. Whether it's guilt, anger, love, loss or betrayal. Change is never easy. We fight to hold on and we fight to let go."

Unknown

I have been accused of being cold and off putting when I discuss my boys.

I have grieved for what I have lost. There are so many firsts that we never got to experience. It may seem simple or trivial to others, but we never had the parent experience of a prom, a high school graduation, or teaching our kids to drive. We didn't get to experience "normal teenage things." Our journey was very different, right from the very beginning of the teen years. I actually spent time grieving for what was lost. Earlier, when I referred to the pile of crap that I had to work through, that was my grieving process. At this point I felt as though I had permanently lost my boys. I had days where I couldn't get off the floor, crying my eyes out, because they were not my boys anymore. I didn't know who they were; they weren't the boys that I knew and spent years raising. I grieved for who I knew was gone, and at this time essentially they were both gone. I know people who have physically lost their children, and I'm not minimizing or saying it's the same thing. All I can say is that it was incredibly painful, and there was no promise of a turnaround in the future and as a result my life was forever changed.

There's an ongoing pain that can't be resolved. I know that when I lost a family member, and went through the first birthday, and Christmas it's all new, but it's how it's going to be moving forward. Our life was unpredictable. We spent five years basically living on egg shells not knowing what was going to happen next, who was going to come home? Were we going to get a dreaded phone call in the middle of the night? Was anyone going to come home for a birthday? What was Christmas going to look like and what bomb was going to blow up?

Everything is different now. It's not easy, fixed or changed, it is just different. I have learned to change the lens so I see life in a new light. I certainly grieved for what we lost and I also grieved for that story of what I thought our life was going to look like. The plan I made for our life, the plan that everyone has for their life. The plan of healthy, happy kids and a life full of memories, love, happiness and opportunities. I had to let myself grieve in order to let go of it. I had to feel the pain of it with no fixed agenda or timeline. I had to remind myself that this was part of my boy's journey's.

Maybe they will go on to impact someone else, maybe they will have this stumbling block for the next couple of years and maybe they will find their way, maybe they won't, I don't know. It is not for me to answer. In fact it truly never was mine to answer.

My husband and I have talked about this and agreed that if they came back and said, "I don't want to do this anymore", we would be there for them in a heartbeat. We could do this because we're not holding onto anger anymore. However, we still wouldn't change our boundaries, rules and expectations.

We may have made our share of mistakes in this process, but our rules didn't change in the whole five years that we were in the chaos. What changed was how strictly we decided to follow them. Our expectations never changed, they were the same all along.

We have had moments of massive growth, moments where we can have real, respectful conversations with our kids. I am so grateful for these moments and our candid conversations. I will take it without any expectations. It just is. I will take each day as the present day and if the shoe drops then I will stop and pick it up. I won't plan on the shoe dropping because that is living in tomorrow.

I learned to live now. I believe we all need to learn to live in present moment. I don't think you can do that until life forces you to. Amidst all the chaos, pain, hurt and loss, I am grateful for the lesson of learning the power of this present moment.

Conclusion

Letting Go of the Why

"Life can only be understood backwards; but it must be lived forwards."

Soren Kierkegaard

This is one of my all time favourite quotes.

Life can only make sense when we look in at it in reverse. It doesn't always make sense yet sometimes when we look back we can see how the dominos added up to bring us to where we are today.

We tend to spend so much time questioning and looking for justifiable explanations as to why things happen the way that they do.

The **WHY** is only important when we are driving toward our goals, when we are working for a purpose. In this example, the why can keep us grounded and focused.

When we use the word why for judgement, justification or jealousy, it can be paralyzing. It will keep us stuck in our challenges, unhappy, and not living the life we are meant to live. It is a complete waste of time, energy and precious resources. Asking why keeps us tied in the past reliving painful memories and missing the joys of the present moment.

I don't know why my boys started drugs when they did or why it escalated to the level that it reached. Truthfully it doesn't matter anymore. The why is irrelevant.

The word **WHAT** is all that matters.

What is my next step?

What is my choice for my life?

What do I want to create in my life?

What makes me happy, fills my cup to overflow?

The word WHAT grounds me and reminds me that it is not all about me? Life is happening for me not to me.

What legacy do I want to be remembered for?

The WHAT is everything!!

What I do know is that I can only love others to the extent that I love myself. In order to love myself I must live in gratitude for every single lesson and experience that I have encountered. I must love the good, the bad and the ugly. All of it. Hate is not an option anymore. I choose to spend my energy differently. I choose to love.

What I do know is that I love my boys. They're incredible human beings who were given to me for a reason.

They have taught me more than they will ever realize. They are here for a purpose. They will tap into their own gifts, be their own person and do what they are here on this earth to do. Regardless of where their life leads, I will love them no matter what.

Our story isn't over. It is ongoing and it will always be a work in progress. And so will yours.

Resources

Breaking the Habit of Being Yourself...How to Lose Your Mind and Create a New One, Joe Dispenza, Hay House Publishing, 2013

Letting Go, The Pathway of Surrender, David R Hawkins, Hay House Publishing, 2013

Love Warrior: A Memoir, Glennon Melton Doyle, Flat-iron Books, 2016

Psycho-cybernetics, Maxwell Maltz, Pocket Books Publishing, 1989

Rising Strong: How the Ability to Reset Transforms the Way We Live, Love, Parent and Lead, Brene Brown, Spiegel & Grau Publishing, 2015

Stay Close: A Mother's Story of Her Son's Addiction, Libby Cataldi, St. Martin's Griffin Publishing, 2010

The Four Agreements, A Practical Guide to Personal Freedom, don Miguel Ruiz, Am-ber-Allen Publishing, 1997

The Gifts of Imperfection, Let Go of Who You Think You're Supposed to Be and Em-brace Who You Are, Brene Brown, Hazelden Publishing, 2010

The Power of Vulnerability, Brene Brown, TED Talks, 2011

The Universe Has Your Back: Transform Fear to Faith, Gabrielle Bernstein, Hay House Inc., 2016

What I Know For Sure, Oprah Winfrey, Flatiron Books Publishing, 2014

About the Author

For 25 years Marsha Vanwynsberghe has worked as a Kinesiologist and Personal Trainer. She coaches and mentors people to make physical changes in their bodies and emotional transformations in their lives.

Due to her life altering family crises, Marsha learned through first hand experience the power of personal growth, expanding mindset, consistent exercise and clean nutrition. Many situations occur that are not part of our life plan and no one plans on adversities such as substance abuse issues in their family.

Marsha found her passion and purpose to inspire and assist others to create change in their lives. She coaches people to learn the tools to live a life unstuck. She found the gifts in her adversities and now speaks openly on issues that no one wants to discuss.

Marsha is sharing her lessons learned and her story through coaching clients, speaking and workshops. She is also a featured author in the book titled, "Influence", by Gerry Visca, as well as a co-author of the book Shine: Inspirational Stories of Choosing Success Over Adversity (Volume 2).

Marsha lives in Waterloo, Ontario with her husband Brad. She has two sons. She loves to travel and is on a mission to share these lessons to help others live more fulfilled and impactful lives.

Connect with Marsha at www.marshavanw.com

Listen to Marsha's podcast, "Own Your Choices, Own Your Life" at www.marshavanw.com/podcasts.

Made in the USA
Columbia, SC
15 March 2018

"Marsha's story is a courageous journey of hope, belief and inspiration. Her insights will crack open reader's hearts and help them find the answers dwelling deep within."
GERRY VISCA
TRANSFORMATIONAL NOVELIST

Marsha Vanwynsberghe's story is one of a mother who fought the system to try to save her kids and her family from the downward spiral of substance abuse. She relentlessly searched for answers, solutions and support. In her search, she found thousands of other parents who were also dealing with substance abuse issues and their teens. Parents who were hiding from the world, living with shame, guilt and embarrassment for choices that were not theirs to own. Marsha decided to speak up, share what she learned and create a light of hope for other parents.

This book is for every parent who is searching to:

- Be present for your kids and not lose yourself in the process
- Parent with love and let go of the expectation of perfection
- Learn the power of personal and energetic boundaries
- Surrender what you can't control and own what you can
- Let go of the judgement of self and others
- Stop letting fear drive the wheel
- Find the gifts in adversity
- Build your confidence, clarity and courage
- Recreate the relationships in your life with yourself, your partner and your children

Marsha Vanwynsberghe is a Life Adversity Coach, Author and Speaker. She coaches and mentors people to make physical changes in their bodies and emotional transformations in their lives.

Due to life altering family crises involving primarily substance abuse, Marsha learned through first hand experience the power of personal growth, expanding mindset, consistent exercise and clean nutrition. Marsha is now on a mission to be a difference maker to inspire others to see and believe in themselves, regardless of their life adversities.

www.marshavanw.com

ISBN 9781988925059

90000 >

9 781988 925059